ELISE OLMSTEAD

The Myth and Mystery of
Seattle's "Queen of the Bootleggers"

ALBERT GIDARI

ELISE OLMSTEAD

DEDICATED TO

Patricia McFarlane, daughter of Elise and Roy Olmsted

TABLE OF CONTENTS

PREFACE

This is the first book to look at the life and times of Elise Olmsted, wife of Seattle's "Gentleman Bootlegger," Roy Olmsted. This is how she is always described – "the wife of a bootlegger" – but it is not how she should be defined or remembered. She was an independent woman, ahead of her time, confident, strong, strong-willed, an entrepreneur at a time when women worked more in the home than the office. Yes, she was married to Roy Olmsted, but it is arguable as to who influenced the other the most. Still, it is fair to ask whether you would be reading this book at all but for Roy? But for Roy. That is both a question and an answer when it comes to evaluating the life of Elise.

If you don't know about Roy Olmsted, he was the baby-faced, garrulous Seattle police lieutenant who, well before he met Elise, got caught landing a load of bootleg liquor on a deserted beach north of Seattle in the early days of Prohibition. Dismissed, fined and freed of his day job with the police, he built an empire illegally importing and distributing premium bonded whiskey and spirits throughout the Pacific Northwest. He did so without the guns and violence that typified the Prohibition experiment in the rest of the country. Instead, he paid off and bribed those in power to take a sip and look the other way. This business-like approach to running liquor earned him the nickname the "Gentleman Bootlegger."

At the peak of his success in 1924, Roy divorced his first wife and married Elise. She was the much younger, "vivacious," stylish and exceedingly attractive English woman from London who had become the bookkeeper for his bootlegging organization. It is easy to see why Roy fell for her, and why she fell for Roy, the older, wiser, charming man from a different world.

The newspapers crowned her "Queen of the Bootleggers." She became an endless object of fascination, speculation and interest for reporters. It sold newspapers. But was she the brains of Roy's outfit? Was she an informer for Prohibition agents before she married Roy? Did she illegally enter the country, leaving behind a husband and child in Canada before she met Roy? Was she a spy for England in World War I or for the U.S. in World War II? Did use her radio broadcasts of bedtime stories for children to send coded messages to rum running ships?

She never deigned to dispel the myths or mysteries about herself or her past. If anything, she cultivated them. Only once did she publicly deny an accusation. She denied ever having been married before Roy, but it was what she didn't say about abandoning a family in Canada that told the real story as you will see. Elise was a woman who wanted to erase her past, not illuminate it, and in her mind at least, she had good reason to do so.

Elise once quipped to a reporter that she might write a book about being a bootlegger's wife. She never wrote it. She had other achievements and accomplishments that occupied and defined her life. If she had penned the book, a better title might have been "Never Just a Bootlegger's Wife."

Until now, Elise's story has never been fully or accurately told. Finding the real Elise was not easy. It took a lot of digging into her past, her family history, finding the right public records, or not finding them in some cases, some lawyer's intuition, and finding and convincing her daughter and grandchildren to talk to me. The last thing actually was the easiest because they were eager to learn more about Elise's life too. Genealogical research makes privacy lawyers like me queasy, so I am grateful for the support of Elise's family.

AUTHOR'S NOTE ABOUT THE "OLMSTED" NAME

Is it "Olmstead" or "Olmsted"? Roy's case before the Supreme Court was styled *Olmstead v U.S.*, 277 U.S. 438 (1928). It was captioned the same in the U.S. Court of Appeals for the Ninth Circuit and in the District Court for the Western District of Washington. No one knows why. But there is no question that Roy was born "Olmsted," or that it was the family name used by Roy himself, his parents, his siblings, and all those who knew him. When Roy married Elise in 1924, he wrote his name as "Olmsted" on the marriage certificate.

Indeed, the "Olmsted" spelling traces back through Roy's direct lineage to the 16th century. When Roy's father moved the family to Seattle at the start of the 19th Century, they came with the name "Olmsted." Roy's father and sister Sallie started the family real estate business in Seattle under that name, with countless ads appearing in the newspaper for Olmsted Realty over almost 40 years.

So what changed? No one went to court to change the name. Patricia and her children believe Roy's family insisted on him using the different spelling in an effort to distance themselves from Roy's bootlegging crimes and reputation. It would be understandable, if true, because Roy had two brothers who remained in good standing on the Seattle police force. However, inexplicably, the names are spelled both ways by various family members themselves, throughout their lifetimes, in directories, newspapers and family documents. If there was any intentionality to the spelling change for Roy, particularly around the time of his legal troubles, there does not appear to be a record explaining it.

Apparently, the spelling confusion goes back a long way. In 1912, in the *Genealogy of the Olmsted family in America: Embracing the Descendants of James and Richard Olmsted and Covering a Period of Nearly Three Centuries, 1632-1912,* the author notes the confusion but has chosen to use the "'Olmsted' spelling throughout the book despite the fact that it has become common among many descendants to use 'Olmstead.'" I have done the same unless "Olmstead" is otherwise used in a specific quotation.

PART I

ELISE, BEFORE ROY

Looking for Elise

Elise's early life has always been a mystery. Researching her early years before she married Roy Olmsted, Seattle's "Gentleman Bootlegger," was complicated by the numerous names, and the various spellings of each, that she adopted throughout her life. When the government indicted Elise and Roy in 1924 for conspiracy to violate Prohibition laws, the government let it be known that Elise used numerous aliases – names such as Elsie Campbell, Vivian Potter, and Elise "Paiche." Apparently, even the government didn't know her real birth name.

Her marriage certificate to Roy in August 1924 added a new name to the mix: Elise Caroline Parchè. Knowing that she immigrated to Canada from England in the Fall of 1919, it didn't take long to find her Canadian immigration record, but that added yet another name: Elisa C. Parsche. The record showed that she was just nineteen and that she was going to Vancouver, British Columbia, "to be married," to P. Campbell. Now there was a link to one of her alleged aliases: Elsie Campbell.

Working backwards from the date of her immigration, she would have been born in October 1899, and there it was in the birth registrations in London – a birth record, albeit under yet another name: Elsie Carolina Parsche. That was her real birth name – Elsie, not Elise. She was born on October 20, 1899, to Ignatz and Caroline Parsche. From there, the entire Parsche family was relatively easy to identify using genealogical research tools. In both the 1901 and 1911 England Census, she is identified simply as "Elsie Parsche." And with that, Elise's early life began to come into focus.

So when did Elsie become Elise? Having grown up as "Elsie," upon her Canadian immigration in 1918, she seems to have tried out the name "Elisa." It is unlikely that "Elisa" was a scrivener's error by immigration or ship personnel for "Elsie." The spelling shows intentionality. We do not know the name she used during the brief period she lived in Vancouver, British Columbia, however, records from her first crossing into Washington in 1920 list her as "Elsie Campbell," a name she also used for her second border crossing in 1921.

It is not until her marriage to Roy in 1924 that the name "Elise" appears on an official document for her. But the name "Elise" does appear on another birth record – the birth record of her sister Lily's first child, born in 1922. If Lily named her child after Elise, as everyone in Lily's present-day family believes,[1] then it suggests that in fact, our Elise used the name earlier and her family, or at least Lily, was aware of it. Whatever the case, it seems that "Elise Parchè" made her public debut in Seattle when she married Roy, but Elsie Campbell did not go away as everyone else knew her as Elsie Campbell before the marriage.

The story of Elise's early years before leaving England is limited to the available public records. Unfortunately, Elise did not discuss her childhood with her friends or family while she was alive, and she left nothing behind to illuminate her early years. Elise's daughter Patricia has said that her mother almost never talked about her life or family at all, even the fact that she grew up in London, England: "She wouldn't even say if she had ever seen the changing of the guard at Buckingham Palace."[2]

Indeed, Patricia believes that her mother actively destroyed a number of documents and photographs that revealed more, or too much, of her past: "For whatever reason, this lady did not admit her past, and tried to eliminate information about it." Among the things that "disappeared," according to Patricia, was Elise's confirmation bible. It had been sent to Patricia by her uncle, Elise's youngest brother John.[3] Indeed, it seems that Elise saved nothing from her youth, nothing about her family, and nothing otherwise about her days before marrying Roy Olmsted in 1924.[4]

At least we found her real name and know where she came from, who her family members were, and how she came to America. From there, we can now fill in the story of her early years in more detail.

Elise's Early Years

"Elsie Carolina Parsche" was born in Holborn, London, on October 20, 1899, to Ignatz and Carolina Parsche.[5] She was not exactly born English. Both parents were German immigrants who initially settled in a vibrant German community in Edinburgh, Scotland. By the time Elise was born, they had moved from the predominantly German community in Edinburgh to a similar, mostly German community in Holborn, London. German probably was spoken in the home because Elise later in life was fluent in it.

Her father Ignatz was born in Gersdorf, Austria, in 1851. Ignatz, his older brother, Franz Xavier, and younger brother, Hermann, emigrated from Germany to Edinburgh in about 1865. The move was likely for economic reasons, joining a large migration of Germans from the Continent to England and Scotland in the late 19th century.

Ignatz was a "flesher" or butcher, as was his younger brother Hermann. Ignatz's older brother Franz went to work in a glass factory and then immigrated to Chicago in 1874 where he became famous as a decorative glass engraver and manufacturer.[6]

Ignatz met his first wife, Anna Elizabeth Hohmann in the German community in Edinburgh. She was born in Germany about 1850, but it is unclear when she emigrated. They married on December 1, 1871. He and Anna had 4 children – Christian Otto (1873), Julia (1877), Franz (1881) and Alice (1886). According to the 1881 Census, Ignatz had become a successful "master flesher," which is to say, more than just a butcher, employing several butchers and successfully managing a meat business.

Unfortunately, Anna died giving birth to Alice in 1886. Somehow Ignatz managed as a single parent for several years, but at some cost. His oldest son Christian Otto was indentured in the Merchant Navy in 1888 at just 14 years old.[7]

In 1890, Ignatz remarried another German woman named Carolina Stahl. The family moved to St. Nicholas, Deptford, London, where he continued in the butcher business.[8] Ignatz's younger brother, Hermann, continued to work with him in the business and lived with Ignatz's family until he later married.[9] The Parsche household also included three children from Ignatz's first marriage: Julia, now 13, Franz, age 10, and Alice, the youngest at age 5.[10]

Ignatz and Carolina had their first child, Lily, in 1891. Four more children followed over the next ten years: Wilhelm Johann (1894), Hermina or "Minnie" (1896), Elise (1899) and Carl Johann (1901). Sometime between 1890 and 1900, they moved to Holborn where Elise was born, and then again later to Islington, another suburb of London.[11]

Only one early photograph of the Parsche family has turned up, and it came from a descendant of Elise's sister, Lily. The family photograph is taken at the turn of the 19th century with, we think, Elise as a baby. The photograph is included in this book.

There is some question in the family whether the baby in the photograph is actually Elise or her younger brother John, making Elise a no-show at the age of two, which seems improbable. More likely, the baby in the photo is actually Elise, taken before John was born. In any case, there are no other early photographs of the family or Elise as a child.

None of Ignatz's children from his first marriage were listed as living in the household by the time of the 1901 census.[12] Julia was married and living in Islington. Otto was in the merchant navy. Franz enlisted in the militia in 1899 and served until discharged in 1903. His militia application stated that he too was a butcher by trade, like his father, and lived in Islington.

Alice is the odd census entry in 1901. It shows her "visiting" a family in Stokes Newington about 2 miles from Islington. It is unclear if she was working in the household there or boarding. No member of that family is related to her or within 10 years of her age. Alice, who would be 26 at the time of the 1911 census, is not listed again in either that household or living with Ignatz.

Whether Elise's half-siblings played any part in her life growing up is unclear. To call them half-siblings is a misnomer because, in the household, they were sister and brother, having been raised together as one family. Due to the age differences, Elise's older siblings may have had a closer relationship with them. For example, Elise's older brother Wilhelm listed both Alice and Julia as his half-sisters and next of kin in his enlistment record in 1915.

In any case, Elise seems to have had no contact at all with them later in life. She never mentioned the existence of these relatives to her own daughter or grandchildren – a pattern of ghosting family members discernible over time with Elise. Elise's own daughter was unaware of any of these relatives or family history.

Elise's father died in 1910, leaving Carolina a widow at 52 years of age. Sometime after his death, she moved the family from Islington across England to Seacombe near Liverpool, some 200 miles. We don't know why they moved. There is no indication that Carolina had family in the area, but Liverpool had a sizable German population, so it is possible. Liverpool was a cosmopolitan city with a large German community. There were pork butchers, bakers, and other familiar businesses and that many have been the attraction.

They took up a household at 10 Palatine Road, in nearby Seacombe. Lily was 19; Wilhelm, age 16; Minnie, age 15; Elise, age 11; and Carl Johann, age 9.[13] How they made ends meet after the death of Ignatz and their move to Seacombe is a mystery. But it got worse. Carolina died in 1914 when Elise was just fifteen. Wilhelm at least was working by then as a millhand, but then World War I broke out in July of that year and everything changed.

The War Years

There were about 53,000 Germans living in England when World War I started. Many of them left for Germany in the face of rising anti-German sentiment. Others with British family ties or businesses remained. It had to be a nervous time for the Parsche family. Anti-German sentiment was rising to a fever pitch.

The sinking of the *Lusitania* by a German submarine on May 7, 1915, resulting in 1,198 deaths, unleashed the mob throughout England. Virtually every German-owned shop in the country had its windows smashed. In London alone, 1,950 properties were attacked. The riots were especially bad in Liverpool, the home port of the *Lusitania*. One newspaper reported: *A large pork shop at the corner of Smithdown Road and Arundel Avenue had been absolutely wrecked, all the windows had been smashed and the stock commandeered or thrown into the street.*[14] Another noted: *The rioting was naturally worse near the docks, for in many of the little streets thereabouts every second butcher's or baker's shop is German."*[15]

Although not directly applying to Germans born in England and therefore British citizens, the Aliens Restriction Act prohibited noncitizen Germans from moving more than five miles and required registration with the police. The Act also eliminated all German newspapers and clubs. A series of other measures closed down German-owned businesses in Britain and confiscated property and assets without compensation for the owners. And then there was the policy of internment of German males of military age (17–55) and deportation of "enemy aliens."

Even if the law treated Germans born in England as having the rights of Englishmen, the mob seldom differentiated between German "aliens" and those Germans born and raised in England. And it didn't matter that the German resident had a son serving in the Army or not.

Wilhelm enlisted in June 1915. His departure left older sisters Lily and Minnie to care for Elise and her younger brother Carl. We don't know if or how the riots affected the Parsche family directly. We don't know if Wilhelm stopped using his given name because of the rising anti-German sentiment before the War, or whether it was a natural Anglicizing of his name to William at an earlier age. The same is true for Carl Johann who later went by John.

The family paid the ultimate price as Englishmen when William, a private in the Cheshire Regiment, was killed in action in 1916 in Flanders. The Birkenhead News on Wednesday, 15 November 1916, carried the news of William's death (Birkenhead is a small town in Wirral County adjacent to Seacombe):

Killed Instantly. Miss Parsche, of 10, Palatine Road, Seacombe, has received the sad news that her brother, Pte. William John Parsche, of the Cheshire Regt., was killed in action on October 7th. He was only

19 years of age, and previous to joining the Army, in June last, was employed with Messrs. Bibby and Sons, Liverpool. Pte. W. H. Young writes "Dear Miss Parsche, It is with much regret that I write these few lines to you. By now you should know the fate of your brother Will from other sources, but I, as one of his chums, feel that I should send a few words of sympathy to you. Will was killed instantly by a shell, and suffered no pain whatever. He died doing his duty as bravely as any soldier could possibly be. He was most cheerful even at the worst of times, and I shall miss him sorely, but not the same as you will miss him. If you should want further information I would only be too pleased to give you all the assistance I possibly can. I must conclude, trusting you will bear your trouble bravely, and accept my deepest sympathy." The Rev. J. D. Hepple, Chaplain, writes:- "Dear Miss Parsche.—I expect you have received the news of your brother's death. He was killed in action on October 7th. May I offer you my heartfelt sympathy with you and yours in your loss. I pray that God may strengthen you with the power of His Holy Spirit in your hour of sorrow. These brave heroes of ours are fulfilling the great precept of our Lord. "Greater love hath no man than this that a man lay down his life for his friends.—Yours in deepest sympathy. We who knew him, mourn the loss of a gallant comrade."

Lily was named William's beneficiary and received the Widows and Dependents of Other Ranks pension upon his death. A typical pension at the time for an enlisted man was the meager amount of 10 to 30 shillings per week. [16]

There is no record of how William's death affected Elise. She lost her older brother to war yet neither Patricia nor her children ever heard about this loss. Lily and Elise did their part for the War effort at home. Lily, a talented musician, actress and singer, entertained the troops in Liverpool. Elise was also musical, talented and beautiful and joined her sister in performing.[17]

Elise also claimed to have "served in a recruitment office" in Liverpool from 1915 to Christmas Day in 1918. As proof, she said: "I have a letter from Sir Aukland Geddes, former British ambassador, thanking me for my war service."[18] Geddes was Director of Recruiting at the War Office from 1916 to November 11, 1918. The implication of Elise's statement was that she was known personally to Geddes and had received a personal letter of reference or introduction. That was not the case.[19]

The actual Geddes letter, dated November 11, 1918, the date the War ended, was among the few documents and materials Elise kept during her lifetime. But it was not a personal letter at all, but rather a general letter from Geddes, thanking all of the "official and clerical staff" of the Ministry at Headquarters or in the Regions for their service and announcing the closure of the Ministry of National Service effective that date.

Of course, anyone who read the letter at the time would have understood the general nature of the correspondence. It was a testimonial of sorts to the effect that anyone who served under Geddes had done creditable work during the War. But there is no record of Elise's service at all as an actual government employee in recruitment or otherwise. Remember, she was all of sixteen or seventeen at the time.

Assuming Elise did, in fact, volunteer in the recruitment office in some capacity, however, such a letter would have been deserved and would have been of help to her after the War. But there is no doubt that she exaggerated its importance.

One other wartime story involving Elise needs to be addressed. It is one of the enduring myths about Elise that she was a "spy" during the War. Elise's daughter Patricia recalled hearing at some point that Elise had "served" in World War I. She wrote the following in 1993 to Philip Metcalfe, a historian writing a book about Roy's Prohibition days:

> *At the time of WWI, Elise went into the service of the British Army and received some type of recognition or medal for what she did. It had something to do with her knowledge of German. I saw the medal of which she was proud.* 20

Metcalfe included and expanded upon Patricia's memory about Elise in his book, writing that "[d]uring the World War her knowledge of German brought her to the attention of the British military, for whom she performed meritorious intelligence work and was awarded a civilian medal."[21]

In fact, there were no civilian medals awarded by the British government for non-campaign related civilian service during World War I. Some civilians who served in auxiliary roles alongside the military might have been awarded campaign medals, but Elise is not listed on those Medal rolls. We don't know what Patricia may have seen among her mother's possessions in those early days of her youth – perhaps it was the Geddes letter – but there is no medal, personal letter of commendation or other recognition among Elise's possessions today.

Nor are there any records to show that Elise was employed as a civilian by the military or other governmental agency in an intelligence capacity. Again, at the young age of 16 or 17, as the War was winding down, it is unlikely that anyone in the military would have sought Elise out to perform intelligence work. Apart from Patricia's recollection, there is no evidence that Elise told others about such work, or ever bragged about or suggested that she served in an intelligence capacity during the War.

As Patricia herself has noted many times, her mother did not discuss her past with her, so how or from whom Patricia heard this tale is uncertain. But Elise was a master at cultivating an image of mystery. If such a story had gotten around somehow, she probably would not have denied it; indeed, she would have liked it a lot.

So what explains the persistent myth? One of Patricia's sons recalls Patricia telling him that Elise did have wartime service, which Patricia described as "watching or informing on members of her community, probably people of German descent."[22] In short, she may have been an informant for the government, reporting on anti-War activities in the German community. In other words, Elise's efforts may have been off-the-books so to speak.

Germany had an extensive spy network throughout Europe, including in England. Counterintelligence was a priority for both governments. MI-5, England's main counterespionage agency, certainly recruited and relied on informants.[23] The British government often paid informants for their information, and it is easy to appreciate that Elise might have needed the money. Not surprisingly, there is no list of informants in either government's records to prove whether Elise was, in fact, an informant or that she ever received any payment.

It is also possible that the myth had a grain of truth in it, but for a different war and a different country. Elise may have volunteered during World War II with the Office of Strategic Services or "OSS" in Seattle. One of her grandchildren recalls having seen an OSS identification card among Elise's possessions, but it could not be found in the materials saved by Patricia.

There was a small OSS office in Seattle during the War, and there certainly was the threat of Nazi infiltration throughout America at the time, so it might have been convenient or even necessary to have German-speaking assistance available. However, just like the British spying claim, she does not appear in the records of the OSS as an employee. Not surprising, Elise never discussed if she worked or volunteered for the OSS, and we have not been able to find the OSS card.[24]

While it is speculation trying to make sense of ambiguous stories, what makes the "informant" story so plausible is that gathering information, networking, and "informing" are traits that will surface again and again in Elise's life story. Metcalfe may have thought Elise's role in the War was more formal than merely a volunteer informant, but his description of Elise later fitting in with Roy's business hits the mark:

> *As an immigrant and former intelligence operative, Elise fit easily into Olmstead's clandestine world. Secretive about her own past, she was expert at finding out about other people and was soon on casual terms with Olmstead's closest associates.*[25]

If nothing else, Elise probably learned at an early age that there was power in knowledge and that it paid to be in the know. Those lessons would later manifest in how she encouraged Roy to use his knowledge of crooked politicians on the take to gain his freedom.

Leaving England, for Good Reason

World War I ended, and soon after, Elise left Liverpool for Vancouver, British Columbia, Canada, in August 1919. Why? The Incoming Passenger List upon her arrival in Quebec City, Canada, says that her purpose in entering Canada was "to be married." Her intended destination was Vancouver, BC., and she lists "P. Campbell, % GPO" in Vancouver, BC, as the contact at her destination.

But running away to get married wasn't her secret. Now we know that Elise was pregnant when she left. As part of the research for this book, her daughter Patricia agreed to take a DNA test to determine whether Elise had been married and abandoned her husband and a child in Canada after arriving from England. The accusation had been made by the government in November 1924 in the newspapers after Elise's arrest with Roy on charges of conspiring to violate Prohibition laws.

Elise vehemently denied the government accusation that she had been married, but she was silent about having or abandoning a child. The omission seemed telling. If true, it would explain a lot about Elise leaving England and her family at such a young age. It might also explain why Elise seemingly severed all ties with her family — could they have known about her pregnancy and opposed her decision to leave for Canada? We don't know, but one thing is clear about Elise - she was a determined, if not obstinate, woman once she made a decision.

Armed with Patricia's DNA results, and using forensic genealogy tools, a definitive match to Patricia was identified – unequivocally Patricia's biological half-nephew.[26] The government's accusation was partially true then, and the real purpose of Elise's departure for Canada was clear - "to be married" to the father of the child she was carrying.

Given that Elise volunteered in the military recruiting office, entertained the troops, and lived in the Liverpool area, it is fair speculation that the father of the child was a Canadian soldier mustering out at the end of the War and returning home to Vancouver. Liverpool was a city choked with troops returning from the War with time on their hands while they waited for transportation home. Even though the Armistice was signed in November 1918, there were over 250,000 Canadian soldiers abroad in January 1919. Liverpool was the embarkation point for many Canadians returning from France. Canada had enough shipping to transport only 5,000 people a week. It would take through the summer of 1919 to get most of the troops home.

If the assumption is correct, it seems likely that the father was named "P. Campbell," the person Elise listed as a contact at her destination on the Canadian immigration form, and the name Elise adopted when she later moved to Seattle. There were a lot of Campbells in British Columbia in 1919, and a lot of Campbells who served in the military, but no "P. Campbell." Of course, Elise didn't know that when she departed for Canada (or it may be that Campbell wasn't even his real name). What is clear is that she was expecting to be married to him upon her arrival. It would not be an easy trip for her across the ocean and continent, pregnant as she was.

Elise's Journey Westward

Elise sailed to Canada on the ship *Tunisian* and arrived in Quebec City on August 25, 1919 after a week at sea. Though pregnant, the journey probably was comfortable enough as summer travel offered calmer seas, warmer temperatures on deck, and longer daylight hours for socializing and activities.

The *Tunisian* was part of the Canadian Pacific Line and was better situated than most Transatlantic shipping. It was christened in 1900 and was advanced for the time. It could accommodate 1,460 civilian passengers on four decks. In magazine advertisements during its commercial career, the *Tunisian* was described as a "Luxurious Cabin Steamer." A photograph of the ship is included in the book.

One passenger's journal offered this assessment of travel aboard the *Tunisian*:

> *"First class travellers [sic] had more spacious quarters, and even cabin class had airier and roomier accommodation. The ship also had hot and cold running water. Closed berths, rather than the open dormitory style of steerage, was another of the major improvements for cabin class on the Tunisian."*[27]

The price of a ticket to cross the Atlantic from Liverpool to Montreal in 1919 varied depending on the class of travel. The most expensive tickets were for first class, which could cost between $200 and $500. Second class tickets were cheaper, costing between $100 and $200. Third class tickets were the least expensive, costing between $50 and $100. We do not know what class of ticket Elise purchased for the trip.

Her undertaking raises another question. How could Elise have afforded the ticket? She was a young woman of just nineteen years old. Both of her parents and her older brother had been dead for several years or more. She was volunteering in a recruiting office and does not appear to have had a paying job. We don't know if either of her parents left any estate for their children as no Will or Probate has been found. But obviously, she found a way, and it shows that she was determined and resourceful even at a young age.

The Incoming Passenger List lists her name as "Elisa C. Parche," age 19, single, occupation "clerk," and religion as Church of England. As noted, her destination was Vancouver, B.C. Having crossed the ocean, Elise still had to make her way across Canada to Vancouver. According to the manifest, a number of other passengers were bound for Vancouver as well as points in between Quebec and British Columbia like Calgary and Winnipeg. Perhaps Elise got some advice from fellow passengers about traveling the remaining expanse.

The distance was almost 3000 miles from Montreal to Vancouver, and it took a minimum of 5 days by train to get there. Presumably, she traveled by rail, but there is no railroad passenger record for her.

The cost of train travel from Montreal to Vancouver in 1919 also would have depended on the class of service and the type of accommodation chosen. However, based on available information, economy class would have cost $50-$60; first class between $75-

$100; a sleeping car between $125-$150. These prices are approximate and would have varied depending on the specific train and route chosen. For example, the Canadian Pacific Railway's "Trans-Canada Limited" offered a more luxurious service with higher fares.

In addition to the fare, passengers would also have to pay for meals and other amenities. Meals were typically served in a dining car, and the cost of a meal would have ranged from $1 to $2. Other amenities, such as bedding and pillows, would have also been available for a fee.

Elise would have been as much as 7 months pregnant by the end of this journey. It is a testament to her fortitude that she made it at all. What she did when she reached Vancouver is unknown.[28] She may have found a private maternity home to assist her with her delivery and the ultimate adoption, but the facts are unknown, understandably.

What we do know is that she did not marry P. Campbell or anyone else, at least according to British Columbia marriage records and by Elise's own admission later.[29] We also know now that Elise had a baby boy on or about October 19, 1919. And we know now that he was adopted by a Washington family and raised in Washington State. He is now deceased, but his son, who took a DNA test unrelated to this book and research, is a conclusive DNA match with Patricia and other family members.[30] That Elise could have had a baby boy and given him up for adoption to a Washington couple who then raised him in Seattle, which Elise likely didn't know, and then moving to Seattle herself where she could have seen him on the street and not recognized him, is just tragic.

"Elsie" Moves to Seattle

Elise first entered the United States on Nov. 13, 1920, under the name "Elsie Campbell," which as we now know was false. She took the *Princess Victoria,* a passenger ship that ran routes between Victoria, Vancouver and Seattle, not unlike the ferry crossings that still run between those ports today in the Pacific Northwest. Every master or commander of a ship had to deliver to immigration officers at the port of arrival a list or manifest of each alien aboard and certify the information identifying the name of the alien and other required information as accurate.[31]

In those days, Immigration officials did not independently verify an alien's name or other information. It was enough that the transport or shipping company would be subject to penalties for providing false information or be required to return the alien if he or she otherwise failed the medical exam or was determined to be an anarchist or other political risk. In other words, the transport company had the incentive to provide accurate information where possible, though the reality is that the shipping company often took the risk, especially on busy routes.

The Certificate of Arrival for Elise stated that she was 5'4" with brown hair and gray eyes and her nationality was English. She gave her permanent residence as Vancouver, B.C., and she stated that she had never been to the United States before.[32] Her occupation was listed as "waitress," and she said that she could read and write, that she had paid her own passage and that she had $50 in cash. Lastly, she confirmed her prior immigration to Canada from England via Montreal in September 1919 on the ship *Tunisian.* These were statutory requirements to be eligible for admission, and based on the records, it all was true apart from the false name.

The Certificate also required the arrival to state her intended destination. Elise provided her destination as 214 Summit Ave., in Seattle, listing her "friend Mrs. B. Cunningham" as her local contact. The destination address provided by an alien is not checked by Immigration officers.

Who is "Mrs. B. Cunningham" and how did Elise know her? There is no B. Cunningham in the 1920 Census at the given address or on any of the adjacent blocks or in any of the local directories.[33] It seems an odd thing to make up, but perhaps she did not want to tell Customs who she was seeing or what she was doing in Seattle. Or maybe the records are just lacking in completeness.

Finally, Elise would have had a cursory inspection by a medical officer with the U.S. Immigration service to confirm that she had no contagious diseases. She was admitted and issued Alien Certificate No. 25907, dated November 16, 1920.[34]

There is no record showing her return to Canada, but she did in fact go back because U.S. immigration records show that, on July 24, 1921, Elise again crossed the border from Vancouver, B.C., to Washington. This time the visit was for a purported stay of 2 weeks, again to see her friend Mrs. B. Cunningham.[35] Elise would deny later that she ever went back to Canada, stating that she entered the United

States in the Fall of 1920 "on a tourist admission [and] never went back."[36]

On the Manifest for this crossing, she answered "no" to the question as to whether she intended to become a U.S. citizen and "no" as to whether she had been in the United States before.[37] And most pertinent to the question of whether she abandoned a family when she came to the United States, Elise stated that she was "single."

At this point, Elise had been living in Vancouver for almost two years and earning a living on her own, at least some of the time under the name Elsie Campbell. The Manifest shows that her last address before entry into Washington was the "Albany Rooms" in Vancouver.[38]

It is unknown whether Elise simply stayed over her visit in 1921 or whether she returned to Vancouver, coming later under some other name or identity, because there is no other immigration record for her. The border was porous in those days, and it would not have been difficult to enter Washington illegally.

Why would Elise later lie about when she permanently moved to Seattle? There may have been a good reason. Overstaying a tourist visa issued in 1920 by six months or more was grounds for deportation, but if the person remained in the country for three years or longer, he or she was exempt from deportation. At the time Elise made her statement on November 21, 1924, in response to government accusations, she may have been acutely aware of the time period necessary to avoid deportation for overstaying her tourist visa and needed to push back her date of arrival in the United States to the earliest entry date to be safe.

In any event, Elise was a full-time resident in Seattle by 1922. A Seattle directory listed "Elsie Campbell" as a hairdresser on University Way. She lived just a few blocks away at 1315 E. 47th St., today the Adelaide Apartments.

From Immigrant to Informant

So as not to bury the lede, no one knows where and when Elise and Roy met, the circumstances of their first introduction, when they became romantically involved, when Elise began working for Roy, and when she became an informant for the government. Some conclusions may be drawn from certain facts, circumstances or mostly reliable accounts, but in the end, no one knows for sure. We only know for sure that Elise became a government informant while working for Roy, and that she ultimately married him. Now, to take each of the questions in order.

Roy may have first met Elise in Vancouver in 1921, and it may have been purely coincidental.[39] As already noted above, Elise was working there as a waitress. Roy traveled frequently to Vancouver to supervise his bootleg shipments. He stayed at the Hotel Vancouver under the name "Potter," a name Elise would later adopt as an alias when she moved into Roy's house before they were married in 1924.[40]

Roy always traveled on these trips without his first wife as she stayed at home with their two daughters, and besides, their marriage had become strained. If Roy had met Elise in Vancouver, it could have been love at first sight, or it could just have been a case of a bright, young woman looking for a job and a change of scenery. Roy may have been the reason that Elise made at least two trips to Seattle, telling Customs authorities her visa was for the purpose of seeing her friend "Mrs. Cunningham." There is plenty of room for speculation, but few facts. What is known is that sometime in late 1921 or early 1922, Elise went to work for Roy as a bookkeeper in his organization.

It would be easier, but less romantic, to believe that Roy and Elise met in Seattle for the first time at some point after she moved there. This was the Roaring Twenties. Elise was young, "vivacious" and loved music. And Roy was distributing to almost every establishment serving liquor in Seattle. Maybe they met at one of the many clubs Roy serviced. Again, plenty of room for speculation, but few facts. But it makes more sense for them to have met in Seattle where she was working in a beauty shop and then went to work for Roy as a bookkeeper.

Once in Roy's employ, she became an informant for the government. While some have said the government "placed" her in the organization to spy on Roy, that claim is not supported by the record. Others, including government agents in the newspapers at the time, have said that she voluntarily came to the government, describing her as "their most reliable volunteer informant."[41] Thinking about Elise's possible role as an informant in World War I, informing on the local German community, it makes some sense that she would volunteer to work with Prohibition agents.

Whether it was by design or luck, having an informant at the heart of Roy's organization was a coup. And Elise was no ordinary snitch. The government acknowledged as much and more when it disclosed her role after the arrest of Elise and Roy in 1924:

Two years ago one of the most frequent visitors at an office that, unknown to the public, was the secret meeting place for local federal dry agents and their "undercover" workers, was a handsome woman.

She was considered by the Prohibition men their most reliable volunteer informant on the operations and intended operations of Roy Olmsted and his men.

She came and went covertly, and her comings and goings were carefully guarded by the agents to prevent her becoming known.

That woman, it was learned yesterday, is the present Mrs. Olmsted.

During the period that the dry office had her confidence, it is said, she often sat for hours explaining minutely the schemes of the liquor ring, and the information thus imparted resulted in a remarkably successful campaign against Olmsted and his operatives that cost dearly in raided whiskey caches, seized automobiles and arrested men. [42]

How successful? Successful enough that through her help the government thought they had the evidence necessary to bring Roy and his West Coast operations down in June 1922. After a successful raid seizing 50 cases of booze, Roy was arrested and charged with being part of a liquor-running scheme that extended from Washington to Los Angeles, California. [43]

Things looked serious for Roy. But a month later, the government sought a continuation of the grand jury because of the disappearance of a material witness – a woman. William Whitney, lead Prohibition agent and assistant prohibition administrator, told the court that it was the government's intention to bring the case before a grand jury the following month. But he declined to name the witness, state the nature of her testimony, when she might be produced, or to disclose any of the other information in the possession of the government.[44] Roy was released from custody the next day when Prohibition Director Roy Lyle declared that the material witness could not be found.[45]

There is no doubt that the missing material witness was Elise and that the tipoff for the raid that led to Roy's arrest had come as a result of her efforts as an informant. Lyle later told the story:

> *She was going to appear before the federal grand jury, she told us one day. The testimony she said she intended to give would have completed a case for us that would have included the whole of the Pacific Coast smuggling ring. Without her testimony the case wasn't clinched.*
>
> *When she left the office that afternoon she promised to return the next, before going to the grand jury room, and to bring us some further information.*
>
> *The next day she telephoned. She said she was with Roy and that she would be with us within an hour. But she did not come. She has never been in the office since.[46]*

Whitney confirmed that he met Elise around June 6, 1922, before she married Roy, and that she told him that she "kept the books for Roy." Elise told Whitney that she had given Prohibition Administrator Lyle a key to Roy's safety deposit box. She also told of liquor caches that had resulted in seizures."[47]

As already noted, we don't know exactly when Roy and Elise began their relationship or under what circumstances, but the June 1922 arrest and near miss grand jury put an end to Elise's informant role. The government would have to build its case against Roy with other evidence, which, it turns out, it was able to do by wiretapping Roy, his lawyer, his dispatcher and others. The surveillance started in July 1924 and continued through the raid on his house in November 1924.

So when did Roy and Elise fall in love? The truth is that no one knows. One story goes that Elise turned to "informant's blackmail" to get Roy to leave his wife so they could marry. Another story has Roy's first wife blackmailing him for favorable divorce terms and that she couldn't stand Elise. The facts suggest that Roy's relationship with Elise overlapped to some degree with the time she was an informant.

It would be easy to make their origin story into a fairytale. As one historian put it, "It was a love match between the older bootlegger and the diminutive flapper from England."[48] That is a fine bit of creative writing and hyperbole, but it is all speculation. Still, the evidence over time confirms a loving relationship. Unfortunately, Elise left no diary or journal, love letters, or interviews revealing the details of their love story. Nor did Roy.

Rather than the certainty of a chronology, perhaps it is enough to remember that she was just 22 or 23 years old and Roy was 36. He was a very charismatic, charming, and confident man, occupying a glamorous world apart from the life Elise came from and was then leading. That Roy was smitten with her is certain. What is less certain is whether Elise put her scruples aside for love or just a good opportunity.

It does beg the question as to why Elise went to work for Prohibition agents in the first place? She drank, she smoked, she was known to curse, she danced, she dressed in the flapper style of the times, and was not adverse to telling lies when it suited her. In other words, she was an unlikely candidate for membership in the Woman's Christian Temperance Union of Seattle! Maybe that's what fooled Roy into hiring her, but it doesn't explain her motivation. In the end, we know she saw Prohibition as a grand hypocrisy. Maybe she had come to that conclusion at the start as well.

PART II

ROY, BEFORE ELISE

ROY ARRIVES IN SEATTLE

The Roy Olmsted that Elise would meet in late 1921 or early 1922 was not the young man of 18 that arrived in Seattle with his family from Nebraska in 1904. To better appreciate the man Elise decided to marry, it is worth looking at Roy's journey to becoming the "King of the Bootleggers" before they married.

Roy came from a long line of self-confident, self-made men and resilient, capable women who moved West with the country over time. His mother was a college graduate.[49] Everyone in Seattle seemed to come from somewhere else and in that mix, Roy prospered:

> *His easy self-assurance brought him to the attention of men of ability and influence.… Olmstead was a born leader, quick and sure in his judgments. He dressed well and employed the vocabulary of a man whose mother was a college graduate. Only his eyes seemed weary. All the Olmstead brothers had ancient, weary eyes.*[50]

Roy's roots ran deep in America, although there is no indication that either he or Elise knew how far or how famously. Roy's seven times great-grandfather came to America in 1632 – just 12 years after the Mayflower landed – and he was among the founding members of the City of Hartford, Connecticut.

Roy's family history contains colonial frontiersmen, Revolutionary War heroes, pioneers, and a few scoundrels. For example, his great great-grandfather Ebenezer Olmsted was appointed constable and tax collector by the town of Ridgefield, Connecticut, and he promptly absconded with the money![51]

As the family moved westward, first to Illinois then to Nebraska, they became farmers. As farming gave out, Roy's father moved to Seattle and went into real estate. Roy took a job as a metal fitter in the booming shipyards, but when construction slumped in 1907, he and his brother Ralph went to work as temporary patrolmen with the Seattle Police Department. The following year they were joined by their older brother Frank. For the next few years, the brothers pounded beats as rookie "harness bulls," a slang term used at the time for uniformed patrolmen.[52]

With his smiling personality, baby-boy looks in a big man body, Roy was immediately popular. Two years into the force, he married Viola Cottle on April 3, 1909. Viola or "Cottie" as she was called by everyone, was 3 months pregnant when they married. Roy's mother was not happy about the marriage, and it caused some hard feelings.[53]

But the newspapers were happy for Roy. The Seattle Daily Times reported the news of his marriage:

Roy Olmsted, Telephone Operator, Takes Bride and No Single Men Remain on the Job.

When Roy Olmstead, telephone operator at police headquarters on Captain D. F. Willard's first patrol, reported for duty his morning after a several days' absence and acknowledged that he employed his time to get married, it brought to mind the fact that Olmstead was the only unmarried man on the force at the station until his marriage to Miss Viola Cottle, formerly of Denver, last Saturday afternoon. The ceremony was performed at the parsonage home of Rev. E. H. Lingenfelter, a Methodist Episcopal clergyman of Fremont. Mr. and Mrs. Olmstead at once went to housekeeping in a furnished cottage at 120 West Forty-eighth Street.

In the discussion that was aroused by the marriage of the "baby member" of the force – for operator Olmstead is the youngest man in the department – it was brought out that during the past several years the following members of the headquarters squad have been stung by the matrimonial bee: [....]. Olmstead makes the eighth victim.[54]

Roy and Cottie had two daughters in short order – Vivienne in 1910 and Shirley in 1912. Roy settled into his career as a policeman, and Cottie settled into their home life. In 1910, he was promoted to desk sergeant in the booking office. Roy's Sergeant's photograph is included in this book.

But it was on the police beat that he was most successful. His exploits made for good newspaper copy. The Seattle Star ran this article on page one on November 20, 1914:

Oriental Olmstead, the Brilliant Boy Bull. A Thrilling Tale of Young Cop's Adventures in Chinatown

Sergeant Roy Olmstead, of the Seattle Police Department, has been breaking late print lately with some new stuff. Once he got inside a Chinese gambling den, disguised as a Chink.[55] *Ochre and an eyebrow pencil fooled the Celestials. Another time he got the goods on a joint by making up as a logger. Olmstead fell down hard the other day. An "important" suspect claimed he was stone deaf. If deaf, he couldn't have committed the crime of which he was suspected.*

Olmstead thought the "suspect" was faking. He sneaked up behind him and fired off a revolver. The "suspect" never batted an eye. He really was deaf. Why, the Star wants to know, should Nick Carter, and Diamond Dick, and Old Sleuth, and Old King Brady be immortalized in literature, and the hero of these Seattle exploits forgotten? Answer: They shouldn't. All right, then, professor. A little quivery music, please, and we will present Sergeant Roy Olmstead in the stirring story entitled "Oriental Olmstead, the Brilliant Boy Bull," or "Pinching the Yellow Peril."[56]

The article is accompanied by a photo of Roy – again the baby-face in uniform – set against the backdrop of a large "Diamond Dick" poster that advertised the latest in the popular dime store novel series.[57] The intent was to show that everyone loved Roy, and he was a larger than life character who could be in the movies or the subject of a suspense book. Roy was promoted to Lieutenant in 1919.

When Washington State enacted prohibition in 1916, the Seattle Police Department beat was extended to include the sale, manufacture, keeping, and disposition of liquor. Not surprising, illegal drinking in Seattle soared as did corruption, bribery, and opportunity to make money from illegal alcohol across the entire supply chain. Why Roy got into the business is not known even though the answer seems obvious: everyone around him was doing it and making money:

Olmstead had to face the true nature of his ambition. Never a man to suffer the throes of anguished ambivalence, his decision was quick. He soon began to sell his authority,[58] *and in keeping with his character and the times, he sought high-risk investments for his money. Rumrunning was an easy choice.*[59]

With Roy's experience and personality, it is no surprise that his career in bootlegging took off. While still on the force, Roy became part owner of the Shipyard Services Station, selling "Oils, Gasoline and Accessories" down by the docks where trucks hauling heavy loads late at night attracted little attention."[60] By 1920, he was one of the City's foremost importers of illicit liquor.[61]

But the stakes had gotten higher. In October 1919, Congress passed the Volstead Act, the enabling legislation for the Eighteenth Amendment. National prohibition went into effect on January 17, 1920.

Fall from Grace

At the Meadowdale dock just north of Edmonds, Washington, in the early morning hours of March 22, 1920, two cars waited for an attempted landing of a load of liquor. Federal agents were waiting too and in the ensuing raid over 100 shots were fired at the speedboat delivering the goods. The boat made its escape while the two cars fled the scene in another volley of fire. Roy was lucky; he was in the car that got away, but he was recognized by federal officers. The next day, Roy's parents, family, and friends would see his picture on the front page of the newspaper, not for his police exploits, but as one of eleven people arrested as a result of a raid.

He was arrested at home at 9 a.m. that morning. At first, he tried to say he was home all evening,[62] but that story wouldn't hold water and he knew it. He was promptly dismissed from the police force by noon that day after a quick investigation. The case against him and the others was then turned over to a grand jury. Charges were filed the next day.

The newspapers duly reported the legal maneuvering over the next few weeks but ultimately, Roy and the others pleaded guilty to conspiracy to smuggle intoxicating liquor into the United States. Roy was fined $500 but did not go to jail.[63]

His fall from grace must have hit his wife, parents, and family hard. They watched him go from being a respected police lieutenant to being dismissed from the police force for bootlegging. It had to be hard to stand, especially because the family was religious, conservative and respected members of the community, not to mention that his two brothers Frank and Ralph remained on the police force in good standing. But we can only speculate because there were no statements or interviews at the time from Roy's wife or family, or any journals, letters or other documents that discuss Roy's fall from grace. The absence of public comment by the family on "family business" was the norm throughout their lives.

A Narrow Miss

Free of his day job as a policeman, Roy went full into the bootlegging business. He was encouraged by prominent men who were eager to find a dependable source of bonded liquor:

> *Promises were tendered by figures in power whose identity [Roy]*
> *never revealed. They promised him protection if he would control the*
> *rumrunning trade and keep it free of violence…. He would sell only*
> *genuine bonded liquor – whiskey, beer, brandy and champagne -*

made in Canada or imported from Europe. He would avoid stolen or hijacked liquor. His delivery men would go unarmed. If apprehended, [his] men would not shoot people; they would buy them off.[64]

Roy took advantage of the fact that Canada repealed wartime prohibition in 1919. The liquor that was legal to buy in Canada would sell at a premium in Seattle if it could be smuggled in safely. Roy figured it all out quickly and soon was running liquor from Canada by boat into the numerous docks and landing spots in Washington. And best of all, Canada did not extradite for Volstead Act or Prohibition offenses.

Here's how it worked. A hundred cases of liquor would be bought legally in Canada and then transported by boat to be dropped on one of the many islands just inside Canadian waters. Roy would send a speedboat on a regular run to pick up the liquor and speed back to one of the arranged landing spots along the Washington coast. The load would then be transferred to waiting trucks and driven to various locations in and around Seattle where it was cached for delivery the next day.

A shipment of 100 cases cost Roy $5000. With wages and bribes, the final cost through delivery might be around $7100. The 1200 bottles in those 100 cases brought in $9600, netting Roy a profit of $2500 a shipment, which was roughly what a Prohibition agent would make in a year. It is not hard to see why Roy was so successful. Roy grossed over $200,000 a month for several years while "he controlled an intricate rumrunning empire, and he scrupulously guarded the integrity of his products, selling without adulteration the liquor he brought from Canada."[65]

But that all changed in June 1922. As already noted, Roy had hired Elise as a bookkeeper for his operations. Elise was an informant for the Feds. Roy was arrested and charged with being part of a liquor-running scheme that extended from Washington to Los Angeles, California.[66] Former Seattle police sergeant Thomas Clark – one of Roy's confederates – and four others were arrested in Los Angeles the day before, and 50 cases of liquor were seized by police at the Seattle home of Clark's sister. Apparently, Roy and another employee named Candler Ames followed the liquor to the house, which led to the arrest of Ames. Roy slipped away but was arrested the next day.

Things looked serious, but the end of that story has already been told. Roy had a narrow miss and escaped by becoming seriously involved with Elise. As already noted, we don't know exactly when Roy and Elise began their relationship or under what circumstances, but the June 1922 arrest and near miss grand jury put an end to Elise's informant role. For the government's part, it had to begin building its case against Roy from scratch with other evidence.

Closer to home, the June arrest probably also sealed the fate of Roy's first marriage as Elise held all the cards in their relationship going forward. That Roy was married and had two daughters did not seem to hinder him or Elise. Elise's daughter Patricia has said, "[a]pparently, my dad was somewhat of a womanizer."[67] Patricia was told as much by Roy's brother Ralph who said, "that this was his weakness."[68]

Roy's Marriage to Cottie Ends

In fairness, Roy's marriage to Cottie had run its course by 1922. Cottie lacked a formal education and the finer social graces to fit into Roy's new world of wealth and status. She was a practical woman of her time, a homemaker. Although Patricia never met her, she understood the differences between Cottie and Elise. Cottie could "bake and had mastered the culinary skills of her generation … She knew how to sew [and] clean house."[69] Elise, on the other hand, loved opera, especially Wagner, sang contralto, played the piano, had style and a lovely English accent that added a certain patina of refinement to her. In short, Cottie was everything at the end that Elise was not at the beginning.

There are any number of reasons why divorce became the only option for Cottie – she probably had enough of Roy and the bootlegging, his womanizing in the past, or his ongoing relationship with Elise. Cottie also was a religious person, so the lifestyle that Roy was living must have been difficult to take as well. Whatever the case, enough was enough for Cottie and on January 16, 1924, she sued for divorce on the grounds of "cruelty."

In the 1920s, in Washington State, there were limited grounds for divorce and "cruelty" was one of them. Cruelty could encompass immorality, alcohol abuse, adultery, and a host of other behaviors that Roy would not, under any circumstances, want to come out in a legal proceeding, especially given how much Cottie must have known about his bootleg business.

Her complaint also asked for a restraining order to keep Roy from withdrawing cash and securities from a safety deposit box and from disposing of their touring car valued at $3000. She sought sole custody of their children, Vivienne, now age 14, and Shirley, age 12, plus alimony. And Cottie got herself a very good lawyer to bring the case – former deputy prosecutor John D. Carmody.

Within a month, Roy and Cottie agreed to a divorce settlement that made financial provisions for the two children and gave Cottie exclusive custody. The newspapers reported, "at her own request, [the settlement agreement] does not grant her any share in her husband's property."[70]

Getting custody of the girls and moving them away from the bootlegging trade may have been the most important factor for Cottie. One story suggested that the "two daughters frequently took phone orders for liquor when [Roy] was not at home."[71] Cottie must have been horrified, if true.

One thing should be made clear here, no matter how fed up Cottie was with Roy and his lifestyle, Cottie was not the government's informant as some have mistakenly said.[72] She was never interviewed by the government and did not testify at any of the trials or grand juries. The marital privilege between Roy and Cottie certainly would have prevented such testimony against Roy when they were married. And Cottie's personal interests, and the welfare of her daughters, provided a practical reason for her to avoid cooperating with the government afterwards.

Still, there is little doubt that Roy's "occupation" did not sit well with Cottie, nor did she want the two girls to continue to be exposed to Roy's lifestyle. Soon after the divorce, Cottie moved to Los Angeles with the girls.

To fast-forward for a moment, in June 1926, after Roy's conviction for conspiracy to violate Prohibition laws, Cottie gave an interview to The Seattle Star. The interview ran on Page 1 under the headline "Mrs. Olmsted May Bare Rum Secrets!"[73] The article features a smiling picture of Cottie standing in front of her Santa Barbara-style home in Los Angeles and warns of "rumblings of a new storm about to break in the big liquor conspiracy in the northwest."[74] These "rumblings" the newspaper reported "emanated from the fashionable Hollywood home of Mrs. Viola Olmsted, former wife of Roy Olmstead, convicted 'rum king' of the northwest and one of the leaders among the 200 indicted in the new conspiracy."[75]

What triggered or led to Cottie's interview is unknown, but she plainly wanted to send a message to Roy and anyone who claimed she was paid off in the divorce – she said that she was "now engaged in the real estate business and is making money…. Every cent I have, everything I own, I bought myself."[76] The reporter observed her closely:

> *Seated in the luxuriously furnished living room of the house that she said she bought from the profits of her real estate business, Mrs. Olmstead appeared far removed from such melodrama as rum running and the dangers that beset those who lurk in dark corners in furtive defiance of the law.*
>
> *Comely, with burnished brown hair and wearing a mullah riding habit, Mrs. Olmsted was loathe [sic] to talk at length about the conspiracy case.*
>
> *She was eager however to tell of her two young daughters whom she is educating in high school and in the fine arts. Her whole life is wrapped up in them.[77]*

The resentment that Cottie had against her rival Elise is palpable in the interview. But what were the secrets she was rumbling about? More warning perhaps than rumbling, the reporter says:

> *She admitted today that she has in her possession letters written to her by her former husband in which he names certain higher up persons who were connected with the liquor business. She said also that "it may be when the proper time comes I will reveal their contents, which would startle the northwest."*

> *"I do not want to deliberately do anyone harm" she said "but there may be developments that will force me to make known the contents of these letters, the people they name, and the whole transactions involved."*

> *"I have heard the statement made that I have received a big price for these letters. It is a lie. I have never received a cent, except the settlement that I obtained at the time of my divorce."[78]*

The letters, if they existed, have never surfaced. There were no more interviews of Cottie. She had a new life and wanted to be left alone. Roy's brother Ralph, and Ralph's wife Lulu, maintained their friendship with Cottie. According to Patricia: "They always visited her when they went to California. They were sympathetic, and felt that she suffered a great deal. Under the best of circumstances, divorces are not easy."[79] Cottie would agree, and with that, Cottie effectively disappeared from public view.

By 1930, Cottie was living in San Diego selling cosmetics wholesale. She had a roommate, an older woman, and Viola's two daughters were not living with her anymore. She never remarried and died alone in July 1959 in Los Angeles.

Cottie's two girls seem to have adjusted well notwithstanding the divorce. Vivienne attended Fairfax High School, and her senior picture has the humorous gadfly comment that she "has accepted the position of head mechanic in the garage at Azusa."[80] Shirlee attended Hollywood High School. She must have been popular because the society page of the Los Angeles Times in 1926 noted that she was among the young ladies who attended a "smartly appointed luncheon… where the rooms were fragrant with summer blossoms and ferns."[81]

By 1940, Shirley was working in retail as a saleswoman and living alone, but by 1942, she was working as an "aircraft worker" in Los Angeles and living with her sister. Vivienne had become a nurse. She would later marry in 1946 and move back to the Northwest.

She passed away on San Juan Island in 1976, Shirlie also married and moved back to the Northwest, passing away in Anacortes, Washington in 1984.

That was all Roy's old life now. His new life with Elise foreclosed his past life.

PART III

WHEN MONEY FLOWED LIKE WATER

ROY, ELISE AND THE "DAYS OF OPULENCE"

With his divorce final, Roy was now free, flush with money, and apparently very much in love. The newspapers would come to call these the "Days of Opulence." He purchased a posh home at 3757 Ridgeway Place in the prestigious Mount Baker area of Seattle in early 1924. The ink on Roy's divorce settlement with Cottie was hardly dry before Elise moved in with him in March 1924.

As far as the neighbors knew, Roy and Elise were "Mr. and Mrs. Potter." Roy used the name "Mr. Potter" in Canada, as well as others like "Cosgrove" or "Steele." The house was known as "Mrs. Potter's place" to the neighbors.[82] The landscaper at the Mount Baker home knew her as Mrs. Potter as well.[83]

Roy traveled frequently to Vancouver to arrange and supervise liquor shipments and he stayed at the Hotel Vancouver under the name Potter:

> *On the Canadian side, Mr. Potter was a legitimate businessman*
> *whose entrepreneurial activities put cash in the Canadian treasury.*
> *Canadian customs authorities were impressed by Mr. Potter's energy*

*and by his air of self-assurance as his business concluded, he climbed
into his small coupe to motor south to the Queen City.*[84]

When Prohibition Agent Whitney first met Elise in Seattle in
early June 1922 as an informant, he testified that she went by the
name of Vivian Potter.

Exactly when Elise started using the Vivian Potter name is
unclear. But obviously, it was an assumed name that tied her closely
to Roy – Mr. Potter – one of the names Roy used in business in
Canada. Elise would use the name in many different contexts
throughout their relationship, in both a professional and personal
capacity, without any seemingly nefarious reason. Who knows what
she thought she gained from the subterfuge as everyone over time
came to know her as Elsie, wife of Roy Olmsted.

Roy and Elise hosted grand parties. The society pages reported
that Elise, again under the name Vivian Potter, hosted a concert at
the Mount Baker mansion, featuring singers from "the voice studio
of Amelie Hild in the Yale Building."[85] Among the few keepsakes that
Elise kept was a dance card from a Naval Ball held in honor of Vice
Admiral Frederick Field at the Hotel Vancouver on June 30, 1924.[86]
Field would go on to become First Sea Lord and Admiral of the Fleet.
This was heady company – the new and exciting world that Elise now
inhabited. Three dances were reserved for Roy.

Roy and Elise were married on August 5, 1924, in Port Orchard,
Washington. As already noted, Elise used the name "Parché" on the
marriage certificate, the Frenchified version of her birth name
"Parsche," as opposed to "Campbell," the name she adopted in
Vancouver and in coming to Seattle. Roy must have known

something by then of Elise's past history and her family — the different names alone should have given that away. But how much he knew, or when he found out, is not clear, including about her entire history as an informant for the government.

To pause for a minute in the story, it is fair to ask how Roy could have forgiven or trusted Elise after learning that she had spied on him and his operations for the government for at least a year and that she was responsible for some of his losses and his own arrest in June 1922. "Love is blind" probably is too easy of an answer. A more cynical reason may be that there were enormous risks to Roy and his operations if he didn't marry her. A third response may be that Roy had an enormous capacity to forgive, which he demonstrated repeatedly throughout his life.[87] Or it may have been all three to varying degrees.

In any event, the wedding was a small and simple civil ceremony. There is no wedding photograph, or at least, if one or more were taken, Elise did not keep one. Elise had already set about furnishing the mansion with treasures from around the world when she moved in after Roy's divorce became final.

> *There were rare French tapestries ordered specially for the Olmsted home by a famous New York dealer; an overstuffed davenport and chair upholstered in the much-prized petit point; massive antique chairs elaborately carved and tapestried as for a baronial hall; an exquisite French clock, and a huge French mirror with a carved gold frame which might have graced the palace at Versailles.*

From China there are several beautifully done silk prints, rare Chinese embroidery strips, a tall blue cherry blossom vase and four great Chinese rugs brought from China at Mrs. Olmsted's order.

There is a solid mahogany bedroom suite, ivory enameled, complete even to the beruffled silk spread and the matching rose silk curtains, and an upholstered fiber set designed for the sun parlor which looked down on the beautiful Olmsted garden.[88]

Elise was proud of her house and bragged that "she picked everything myself – no decorators for me. That's why it's all so good."[89] She also bought a piano.

In October 1924, Roy commissioned an appraisal of his household for insurance purposes.[90] The value of the personal property in the home was listed at $115,000, which would be about $2.1 million today. Elise's mahogany piano was made by Apollo Piano Co. of Chicago and was valued at $4,500. It was a "reproducing piano" and came with an electric attachment that allowed "an exact reproduction of the artist's playing without deviation in characteristic of touch, shading of tone or individuality of interpretation."[91] The Living Room held six Oriental carpets, the largest of which was 10×11 feet and valued at $1000.

Elise's jewelry included 4 rings: 1.3k yellow diamond, 1.3k white diamond, 1.17k blue diamond ring paired with a 1.25k blue diamond stick pin and a "princess ring" with 3.25k white stones set in platinum. There was a 2.8k diamond pin, and a Lavalliere with blue stone and small flat diamonds on a platinum chain with clasp. Total value was $6500. Missing from the inventory, however, seemed to be the long pearl necklace that Elise is seen wearing in many of her photographs.[92]

Her wardrobe also is cataloged right down to her "bloomers" and "petticoats." She had a Japanese hand embroidered kimono and another in black satin. Among her "vanity bags" were 8 beaded handbags, which she would become known for knitting during the bootlegging trial. Elise loved her furs. She is often seen in public in her fur coat, a full-length mink coat which the appraisal valued at $1500, and she also owned an ermine jacket valued at $1000, a two-piece Russian sable neckpiece, and one large skunk neckpiece. Her total wardrobe exceeded $7100 and took up seven of the 44 pages of the household appraisal.

It was a busy few months of conspicuous consumption and high living. It was also a busy time for Roy. He called the leading illegal importers and boatmen together one Sunday morning in June 1924. He intended to organize the Seattle bootleggers into a consortium to increase sales and stabilize the pricing, which had been going down due to the huge volume of liquor streaming into Seattle. Roy had figured out the economics of the trade and management of the supply chain. A consortium was formed with 11 partners each putting up $1,000 and Roy adding $11,000, and therefore entitled to 50% of the profits.[93]

The money flowed like the waters of Puget Sound.

A Boat Named *Elsie*

On June 3, 1924, the newspaper reported that Roy was building "the largest and best equipped speed boat ever constructed in the

Northwest…. The vessel is 100 feet long, has triple screws, doubly constructed of cedar and fir, and is capable of developing thirty-five miles per hour."[94] The price was $45,000!

Roy called the boat *Elsie* in tribute to the woman he planned to marry.[95] Perhaps it was a sweet gesture in Roy's eyes, but as far as we know, Elise never set eyes on or stepped aboard the boat. It was built to be a rum-runner, not a touring yacht,[96] and there is nothing to indicate that Elise had the slightest interest in the yacht or boats of any kind.

The boat was being built in the Lake Union Drydock Company yards and a lot of people came to see it under construction, including Coast Guard and Customs agents. Again, there is no record that Elise was among the curious or visited the boat during its construction. To those in the know, it wasn't love that prompted Roy to build the biggest and fastest boat – Congress had appropriated money to build fifteen "rum-chasers" in the same boatyard to try to keep up with the rum-running speedboats.[97]

The boat literally had three, 300-horsepower aircraft engines installed to power it. In her first sea trials, the *Elsie* proved to be overpowered and nearly swamped.[98] A naval architect hired to correct the fault suggested a fix, but before it could be implemented, Customs agents spotted the ship bringing in a load of booze.[99] In the ensuing pursuit, one of the engines burned out. It was undergoing repairs at the Lake Union Drydock when the sheriff seized and sold her for unpaid debts.[100]

Cottie would have enjoyed this turn of events, assuming she knew about it. The seizure of the *Elsie* was the result of an unpaid personal injury damages award due to a car accident on December 15, 1921, where Cottie was at fault. She hit and seriously injured a road-side worker. The worker sued and won a judgment of $14,000 against Cottie and Roy in February 1923.[101] Roy appealed the decision, but the Washington Supreme Court upheld recovery.[102]

The debt for which the *Elsie* was seized was the remaining, unpaid balance of the judgment in favor of the laborer. Roy had paid about $5000, but $10,000 remained. He argued that the boat belonged to Prosper Graignic, his most trusted pilot, and that Roy had just lent Prosper the money, offering the mortgage document as proof. But the Customs' agents had evidence that Roy was the true owner.[103] The boat was sold at public auction. Roy bought it back privately through a third party.[104]

Towards the end of October 1924, the *Elsie* took her final voyage. She was caught in a freak storm north of Seattle and caught fire. Graignic was the skipper of the boat and he and his passenger abandoned ship and made for shore.[105]

The boat sank, and Olmsted's Customs broker, Wilbur Dow, sent a claim to Lloyds of London arguing that Graignic was the sole owner of it and entitled by the insurance contract to payment. The boat was declared a total loss.[106] The claim was paid.

There is something of a bad omen in the sinking of the *Elsie* in the late Fall of 1924. It had the feel to it that the Days of Opulence were coming to end.

Aunt Vivian on the Air

Sometime in early 1924, Roy met a young inventor named Al Hubbard. Hubbard eventually would become the undoing of Roy,[107] but in the early days, he was a wunderkind with his inventions. He was struggling and in debt when Roy met him. Roy obviously saw something in Hubbard because he moved him and his young wife who was pregnant at the time into the Mount Baker house. He set Hubbard up with a laboratory in the basement to work on his inventions and even bought him a car in return for a split of profits on any patents.[108]

But it was Hubbard's knowledge of radio that interested Roy most. Roy felt that his operations were threatened by the increased government enforcement and that he needed a solution to stay one step ahead. Radio might be just what he needed. He reportedly paid Hubbard $15,000 to install a radio station in the spare bedroom of the Mount Baker house.[109]

In July 1924, the newspapers reported that Roy had "added radio to the schemes he has devised to outwit prohibition agents" by installing radio equipment onboard the *Elsie*:[110]

Day and night, while speeding to or from Canadian ports in bold defiance of coast guards and scores of prohibition agents, the daring crew on a new 100-foot speed boat will be kept informed by spies on shore of the movements of officers seeking to trap them.

From a powerful broadcasting station now being installed in Seward Park district, according to the federal agents' information, code messages to guide Olmstead's lieutenants on the speed boat will be flashed. They will be received by the 10-watt radio plant on the speed boat.[111]

The government apparently believed what it read in the papers. They brought Hubbard into the Prohibition office and grilled him. Whitney asked: "You remember the *Elsie? My agents report you built a radio transmitter on her.*" Hubbard replied: "Yes, I built that, but no liquor was hauled on her as far as I know." Whitney pressed: "Don't you think Olmstead was using the radio station to communicate with his boats?" Hubbard admitted it was possible, but denied that he knew nothing about it.[112] The irony, of course, is that the government had issued Hubbard a Class Y Limited Commercial Radio License in July to communicate between ship and land-based stations, and the station continued to operate under an FCC license.[113]

The idea of using radio to direct or tip off rum-running boats was not new or surprising. It would be more surprising if Roy hadn't considered the possibilities. A headline in the Seattle Daily Times in 1925 announced that a "Far-Reaching Espionage System of Rum Runners in East Handicaps Coast Guard:"[114]

Rum runners have established an almost perfect espionage system along the New Jersey and New England coasts to keep tab on government prohibition operations, according to Coast Guard officials today.

The rum informers along the coasts are made up largely of shore raiders. When they see a Coast Guard vessel put out to sea they immediately telephone "the rum headquarters, somewhere in New York," which immediately sounds the alarm by telephone and radio.[115]

Roy also bought two seaplanes and equipped them with radio receivers. The idea was that the planes could keep track of the government rum-chasing boats as well as his own fleet of rumrunners. The plan failed both for technical reasons and the cost of keeping the planes in the air.[116]

In the end, Roy may have used Hubbard's radio setup to communicate instructions to his boats or as an early warning system about government enforcement boats in the area. But it does not seem to have been an important part of his operations. When Hubbard was finally outed as an informant for the government, the detailed account of his exploits in the newspaper concluded "despite popular belief, the radio enterprise of Olmsted never played a part in Olmsted's rum running operations."[117]

The telephone played a much bigger role in moving product and avoiding capture. We know this from Roy's trial and the testimony of John McLean, Roy's chief dispatcher who pleaded guilty in return for not being prosecuted, and the volume of wiretaps the government employed to listen in to the calls. Indeed, not once in the entire trial did anyone ask or answer a question about the use of radio in bootlegging.

The more interesting question is whether Elise had any part in Roy's bootleg radio plans or any other part of Roy's operations for that matter once they were married. It seems unlikely and more, she seems to have pushed Roy to exit the business. Besides, her days were filled with music, literally, as she invited bands to the mansion to practice. There was a steady stream of musicians at her home while she had a radio station to manage.

Elise certainly saw the potential of radio as a commercial business and for its use as a medium for entertainment even if Roy may have had his own plans to use it. She became a partner in the creation of the KFQX radio station with Roy and Hubbard.

Roy, Elise and Hubbard incorporated the American Radio Telephone Company in October 1924.[118] Hubbard owned fifty percent of the stock, Roy and Elise owned the remainder minus 5 shares that they gave to their attorney Jerry Finch.[119] Hubbard installed what would be the first 1000-watt broadcasting station in Seattle on the top floor of the Mount Baker house in a spare bedroom.[120] The new station KFQX went live on the air in early October:

> *Every evening except Sunday, station KFQX began broadcasting at the dinner hour, issuing stock reports, news, and weather. From 6:15 p.m. to 7:30 p.m., Elsie read children's bedtime stories. From 9:00 p.m. to 10:00 p.m. the Earl Gray Orchestra performed concert music.*[121]

Elise is credited with the idea of broadcasting live music. The company rented space in the Smith Tower Building and installed an expensive remote broadcast studio, another of Elise's innovations. At that time, Smith Tower was the tallest skyscraper west of the Mississippi. For the first time, reportedly, the city heard live jazz music from the dance floor of the Butler Hotel.[122] The hour of live music was hugely successful and sponsors lined up to buy advertising.[123]

So instead of an early warning system for bootleggers at sea, Elise's radio plans were a legitimate commercial business and reflected her love of music and the arts, not bootlegging. She wanted her studio to be a place for "artists of the air."[124] Even with the high cost involved in creating the Smith Tower sound-proof studio, Roy indulged Elise. Again, these were the Days of Opulence. The station also provided a small hedge for Roy against the potential loss of his business to government enforcement of the Volstead Act because advertising on the radio was bringing in money, and he was selling radios for the home on the side.

The radio station became Elise's passion. She was the station manager in charge and she was both feet into the business. The station allowed her to blossom as an entrepreneur, a marketer, and an innovator. As one reporter put it:

> *Mrs. Olmsted plunged into the radio work. She toiled long and hard to make the station the outstanding one of the Northwest. Some say she liked the work. . . . She designed a broadcasting room like the rooms used by the singers in Italy for their practice.*[125]

That the radio station was important to Elise is clear enough from the few things she saved from her life with Roy – a trove of letters and articles about the station and its successes.[126]

For example, Elise wrote letters to entice advertisers and partnerships. She wrote the Times-Mirror Company radio station in Los Angeles, and they responded on November 24th to say that Elise's "ideas about operating a broadcast station" were creditable and excellent. The Seattle Chamber of Commerce also wrote in November 1924 to congratulate the new radio station and business. Elise responded on December 17th offering the Chamber airtime, which the Chamber duly accepted.

Some of the correspondence is between the station and the Radio Digest Company, which began publishing the Radio Digest newspaper in 1922. The paper shared industry news and promoted radio products and services. KFQX was newsworthy.

In a letter dated October 10, 1924, Radio Digest asked the station to broadcast a bulletin to its listeners at a certain day and time about minimizing radio interference on the listener's home radio. Such requests were common and intended to improve consumer acceptance of radio. In responding on October 15th and agreeing to broadcast the bulletin, Elise used the opportunity to market the future plans of KFQX:

> *May we draw your attention to the fact that we are pioneering the first Thousand "Watter" on the Pacific Northwest Coast K.F.Q.X. enters the broadcasting field in the Northwest, as bids for favor as the "Daddy of the All."*

> *The location of the broadcaster was chosen as an ideal transmitting station; being located in the Mount Baker District on a high bluff overlooking Lake Washington.*

> *The Studio and offices are on the twenty-first floor of the L.C. Smith building in the downtown district and is connected by private telephone lines. Considerable time has been spent in the draping and acoustical treatment of this Studio to make it perfect in every detail.*

> *A remote control line to the Bagdad Cafe, at Third and Madison St., is completed and in operation, featuring Ray Robinson (late of the Ziegfield [sic] Follies) and his orchestra every night. Other remote control lines are underway to which places we are not allowed to divulge at this time, as we intend to introduce something in the radio world heretofore unattempted.*

The letter is classic Elise, promoting an outsized image of size and sophistication for the station and ending with the hint of mystery.

Not surprising, the Program Editor of Radio Digest – a woman named Grace Hammill – promptly responded, offering to include the station's programming each week in its paper and asking for some photographs of the station to include in an article. A few days later, the Managing Editor of Radio Digest wrote to "Vivian Potter, General Manager of KFQX," to say that they had been unaware of the success of the station in launching a 1000W broadcasting station and that they will run a story about the station in the November 6, 1924, paper. The Managing Editor again asked for photographs of "your studio and station in operation, with engineers at work, and also a good photograph of your announcer at the microphone."

Elise, of course, jumped at the Radio Digest request for a photograph and article about the station.[127] She sent off a picture that would come to adorn the front page of the next Radio Digest edition, a copy of which is included in the center of this book. The picture prompted this reply from Grace Hammill, the Program Editor, who obviously had become a great fan of Miss Vivien Potter:

Dear Miss Potter:

I cannot tell you how surprised the whole office force was when your picture was received. We wondered whether you were a lady, or a man with a strange kind of name.

Then we discovered that you were a girl and a subject for the front page, our astonishment was all it should be. And I said oh well now it will be a small matter to get a woman in the President's chair.[128]

The promised article ran on December 6th and featured Elise on the cover with the caption: "Vivien [sic] Potter the beautiful announcer of Station KFQX at Seattle, Washington. This is a new 1,000 Watt station."

One of Elise's most successful programs was her own "Aunt Vivian" character who broadcast bedtime stories for children each evening. The show was hugely popular. Part of the attraction might have been her charming English accent over the airwaves. Other radio stations copied the idea – Seattle station KJR offered Aunt Bunny – the Story Lady. [129]

Those bedtime stories gave rise to one of the enduring myths about Elise - that her bedtime stories contained coded instructions to Roy's boatmen. [130] Indeed, the government was obsessed with the notion. The newspapers reported that Prohibition agents were looking for hidden code in Elise's "Bedtime" Stories." [131] The government claimed to have carefully recorded the bedtime stories and that they were "investigating whether the innocent fairy tales could be clever code messages used in bootlegging operations." Lyle supported the claim by saying some of those arrested in the raids had radio receiving equipment in their homes. [132] But despite listening to the broadcasts for hours, no one could find any hidden code.

Just as with the claim that Roy used the radio station to send instructions to his cronies, the government provided no evidence in the grand jury or at his trial that coded messages were sent or received by any of those involved in the bootlegging. None of the bootleggers who cooperated with the government against Olmsted testified that they had received coded messages. Hubbard, who became a double agent, never told Lyle, Whitney or others, that Elise's broadcast was being used to direct operations in code.[133]

Elise's daughter, Patricia, also has quashed the notion that there were any codes in the radio broadcasts, quite firmly. In an interview many years after Roy's death, she said "Oh, no, there were never any codes over the radio. They didn't need them. They were too well organized, and had too much money to need something like that."[134]

Finally, the government had Elise on the witness stand during her and Roy's trial and never asked her whether her children's stories were coded messages. She would have denied it of course, but if the government later could prove the fact, they would have had a clear case of perjury to prosecute.

Despite all the early success for Elise, she was about to be crushingly disappointed and all of her work to create a successful radio station would spiral off the air. Prohibition agents were about to raid the Olmsted mansion, disrupt Elise's bedtime story broadcast and ultimately knock KFQX off the air by the end of December 1924.

The government's raid on the Mount Baker home of Roy and Elise on the evening of November 17, 1924, interrupted Elise's bedtime story broadcast. It signaled the end of the radio business, and much more. But even after the raid and with the station going off the air, Elise persisted in keeping the appearance of a running station, sending marketing letters and running the show, but it certainly was all coming to an end. Hubbard complained that his own standing in the radio community had fallen and his business efforts on behalf of the station were unavailing. Roy had to sell or lease the station.[135]

For Roy, the radio station probably always represented just a hard asset and a potential source of cash. For Elise, it was much more. Roy began trying to sell the station and the equipment in early January 1925. KFQX had been off the air for four months when, in March 1925, Birt F. Fisher and the American Radiophone Corporation leased the station for a year with an option to purchase.

The call sign was changed to KTCL, for "Know The Charmed Land." Fisher moved the transmitter to Magnolia Bluff in Seattle and maintained a studio in the New Washington Hotel in downtown Seattle. KTCL went on the air April 29, 1925, broadcasting five hours a day. The station broadcast each day in the early afternoon and again in the evening with programs such as the Western Giant Orchestra directed by Warren Anderson during the week, the Sentinel Program on Saturday nights, and the services of the First Church of Christ Scientist on Sunday nights.[136] Eventually, Fisher changed the station name to KOMO.[137]

The Raid on the Olmsted Mansion

The raid came at 7:30 p.m., on the evening of November 17, 1924, as Roy and Elise were hosting a party at their Mount Baker home. A "posse of federal prohibition agents led by William M. Whitney, assistant director of prohibition"[138] surrounded the house.

Whitney knocked on the front door backed by fifteen agents, some armed with pump action shotguns and sledgehammers. The sledgehammers were for the purpose of destroying the radio equipment should they find any alcohol on the premises.[139] Roy answered the door in person and invited Whitney and the officers into his home. Two agents made their way upstairs to where Elise was in the final minutes of broadcasting her nightly children's story.

She turned to see a tall agent standing in the doorway with a gun. She pushed past him into the hallway to the room housing the radio station and saw another agent holding a gun on her radio engineer. She then went downstairs to one of the two hall phones, picked it up and dialed the police, saying that "she'll have this house full of police in a few minutes."[140]

Whitney pushed her aside and ripped the phone cord from the wall, shouting "This is my party! No one comes here that I don't want." Elise said Whitney "slapped her in the face" when he took the phone away.[141] The party then became a roundup as some of Roy's friends and business associates started coming by and were nabbed in the raid too. Whitney asked Roy what his unlisted number was and Roy gave it to him, saying "I know you know it – you've been listening to me long enough."[142]

Whitney and his wife Clara who, incredibly, accompanied the agents on the raid, began making phone calls, representing themselves as Roy and Elise. They succeeded in luring half a dozen more of Roy's compatriots to the home. When one caller spoke in German, knowing that Elise spoke it fluently, Mrs. Whitney told him to "cut that stuff out and bring out the booze." That was the last call to be answered.[143]

Remarkably, at two o'clock in the morning, with everyone hungry and tired, Elise's cook prepared a big breakfast of ham and eggs for everyone. Then, they all left with the agents to be booked. Roy and Elise rode with Whitney and reportedly Mrs. Whitney, facing backwards in the car, was laughing and waving around Whitney's .45 caliber pistol at them.[144] Roy, Elise and sixteen others were arrested and taken into custody.

The next day, the story was front page news. Seattle Mayor E.J. Brown criticized Director Lyle and the raid as "a grandstand play" rather than enforcing the law.[145] Brown said that the Feds "could raid his home in the same way; come to my home and search it; find no liquor and then telephone to bootleggers who would bring it."[146] Lyle responded acerbically by asking what would anyone expect from someone not in favor of enforcing the prohibition laws.[147]

The affidavit of Agent Corwin in support of the search warrant stated that "he has heard Elsie Olmsted state that there was intoxicating liquor on the premises; and has heard Roy Olmsted state that he had papers and documents relating to the sale and possession of intoxicating liquor on the premises."[148] Corwin also said that he knew that Olmsted and others named in the warrant were involved in the sale and trafficking of intoxicating liquor.[149] His affidavit also tipped the government's wiretapping hand to the public, stating that "liquor was ordered by telephone from the house on July 8 and 9."[150] However, Whitney expressly (and falsely) denied "a rumor that Olmsted's telephone wire had been tapped."[151]

In fact, Roy already knew about the wiretaps.[152] He learned of wiretaps and the breadth of the ongoing investigation against him and his organization months before the raid. Roy's best source of information came from Assistant U.S. Attorney Cliff McKinney. For a few thousand dollars and a steady supply of booze, McKinney kept Roy informed about the investigation, what conversations had been overheard, and who was likely to be arrested.[153] With all that forewarning and inside information, Roy must have been more than angry that the raid came off without warning. He paid good money to be tipped off about raids like this one to those who should have been in the know.

Government Vengeance

Whitney provided the names and descriptions to the newspapers of all those arrested at the mansion, and Roy and Elise topped the list:

> ***Roy Olmsted,*** *"king" of the Pacific Coast Rum trade, heavily interested financially in the Western Freighters, a Canadian concern exporting liquor, owner of smuggling vessels and director-general of the most extensive whiskey trafficking organization in the Pacific Northwest.*

> ***Elsie Olmsted,*** *formerly Miss Elise Caroline Paiche [sic], second wife of Olmsted, known also as Vivian Potter and Elsie Campbell, broadcaster at station KFQX, the 1000-watt radio set in the Olmsted home.*[154]

The government raised the stakes for Elise beyond merely arresting her along with the other guests. She would be charged along with Roy as a co-conspirator, and worse, the government went after Elise with a vengeance. Perhaps it was because Whitney and Lyle did not like being played the fool by Roy or Elise whose marriage derailed their prior bootlegging case against Roy.

The government leaked four damaging stories about Elise to the press in the coverage following the raid. First, the world learned that

Elise had been a government informant against Roy for at least a year and that her marriage foiled their prosecution of him in June 1922 – Roy's near miss. Second, the government alleged that Elise likely entered the country illegally and was being investigated for possible deportation. Third, the government noted, and reporters repeated, Elise used multiple identities and aliases, implying an illegal motive. And lastly, the most scurrilous of all, the government proclaimed that Elise had abandoned a husband and child in British Columbia before coming to Washington.[155] There was no avoiding it now – Elise had become a most interesting news story and she would remain so for years to come.

The story of Elise's tenure as an informant alone was a bombshell. The newspaper called it "Roy's Greatest Coup" in that he outsmarted the government by marrying its main witness against him.[156] The story was picked up by numerous papers around the country – it was the kind of story that sold papers.[157]

Roy must have known all the details of Elise's role with the Prohibition office, so the story could not have been a surprise to him. In today's world of investigative journalism, reporters would want to know every detail about it – which cases did Elise break, who went to jail, and other questions – but curiosity about the scope of her work and her role as an informant inexplicably died down after the initial reports.

Next, the idea that the government was looking into deporting Elise seems absurd given that they had been using her as an informant for over a year. The government knew that she was an immigrant – her English accent gave that much away – and that she was not a citizen when they put her to work. But the deportation threat was real and if carried out would have meant her separation from Roy just as much as the prospect of Roy going to jail.

The government started an investigation "to determine whether her entry into this country four years ago was through legal channels and under circumstances that entitled her to remain."[158] Elise told the Immigration agents that she was British by birth and came to the U.S. from Canada, but Immigration was having difficulty locating the records.

It must have made Elise nervous because she entered the U.S. under a false name – Campbell – at least twice, once in November 1920 and again in July 1921. Immigration officials said that overstay of a tourist entry, which allows a 6 month visit, can be the subject of deportation unless the person remains in the country for 3 years. Elise had been in Seattle for just over three years, assuming the clock started running with her July 1921 entry, but the government was unable to find the immigration paperwork.[159] But Elise told reporters she entered the State in the Fall of 1920 – an extra cushion of time, and false.

Two days later, the government told the press that not only was Elise being investigated for illegally entering the country, but also that she abandoned a husband and child in Canada:

> *Mrs. Elsie Caroline Olmsted, four months' bride of the reputed "king" of the liquor traffic, was reported to Immigration authorities to have abandoned a husband and family in Canada when she came to the United States supposedly in October, 1920.[160] Immigration*

Commissioner Luther Weedin will leave for the border this morning to investigate the matter on his regular tour of inspection.

Desertion Charged

The "tip" from what was said to be a very reliable source that Mrs. Olmsted had deserted a family prior to coming here was considered to be one of the day's most important developments.

Immigration officials for several days have been searching their records to find whether there is any showing Mrs. Olmsted entered this country legally. Yesterday they announced that they had completed their investigation and had found nothing to substantiate it. [161]

Elise responded to the accusations with tears in her eyes, saying:

[i]t is a vile attack upon me and I have no way of fighting back. I have never been married before. I came to Canada from Liverpool in the fall of 1919. My passport was viewed by James G. Balfour, then secretary of foreign affairs. I have a letter from Sir Aukland Geddes, former British Ambassador, thanking me for my war service. I served from 1915 to Christmas Day 1918, in the Liverpool recruiting service.

I landed in Montreal and traveled in Canada a year. I came to Seattle in the fall of 1920 on a tourist admission. I never returned. I never have been married. [162]

Her denial was very helpful in filling in her history. But her silence on the abandonment of a child seemed more of an admission than a denial. Indeed, it told the story. And to cover her past, she lied about "traveling in Canada" for a year as well. Immigration

Commissioner Weedin went to Vancouver to try to determine whether the family abandonment story was true, to no avail.

As with the informant disclosures, the abandonment and the deportation stories fizzled in the press and the government, as well as the newspapers, seemed to lose interest in pursuing them. Having given a false name at least twice upon entry to the country, which would have been sufficient to deport her, but for reasons lost to time, the government never seems to have discovered her real name.

We also do not know the source of the "tip" that Elise abandoned a family in Canada. The records of the Olmsted case do not contain any information about the investigation of Elise, nor do they even reference her time as an informant. Given Elise's penchant for secrecy, it is even more of a mystery that anyone would have known about her child. So it must have been someone that Elise confided in, but close friends or likely confidantes from that time seem few and far between for Elise.[163]

In any case, it had to be a very painful time for Elise. How much Roy knew about her past, and when he knew it, remains uncertain. As already said, he knew she used the alias "Campbell" when they met and thought probably that her name was "Parchè" when they married. Presumably, she told Roy she had never been married, but for what purpose did she tell Roy that she used the Campbell alias? We don't know.

And did she tell Roy about the child when the story broke in the newspapers? Again, we simply do not know. It seems that Roy ultimately found out the truth about Elise's abandoned child. His daughter Patricia has said that Roy told her that Elise had done "something terrible" in her young life, but would not give her more details.[164] It is a fair guess that Roy was referring to giving up her child, which at that time, might have seemed to be something terrible. But no one should judge Elise too harshly who, at nineteen years old, alone in a new country, and apparently jilted by her lover, had to make such a difficult decision.

Moreover, Elise had to live with these public disclosures. The rumors, the stories, the threat of imprisonment and separation from Roy, and the loss of everything that she had in those short days of opulence. To add to her worries, Elise had just become pregnant with Roy's child.

The Parsche Family

L-R: Carolina with baby Elise on lap; Lily, Wilhelm and Hermina

Circa 1900

The Tunisian

The Ship on which Elise Immigrated to Canada

Sergeant Roy Olmstead

Circa 1910

Roy playing the Uke on a boat

Roy's Office in the Mount Baker Mansion

Note the two phone lines on his desk

Elise coming down the stairs in the Mount Baker Mansion

Note the violin on the hall table

*Ruth Elbro, Elise's close friend, until she wasn't, in the Foyer holding the
violin*

Elise Playing the Piano

Elise's Parlor in the Mount Baker Mansion

With Elise's friend Ruth Elbro on the divan

Note: Portrait of Elise above the Fireplace, now with Elise's grandchildren

Close-up of Portrait over Fireplace

Ruth Elbro inscribed photo for Elise

"Yours 'till the last apple falls!"

Elise, one of several photos taken at the mansion in 1924

Elise Closeup

Elise on the Cover of Radio Digest

"Vivian Potter, the beautiful announcer of Station KFQX at Seattle."

Elise Posing

Note the rings on her fingers

Elise - A Sophisticated Look

Elise, Roy and an unknown couple standing in the famous Hollow Tree, a Western red cedar in Stanley Park, Victoria, British Columbia.

Note Elise's luxurious furs.

Roy's mountain of gold, pursuing the Butte Boys claim after his release from prison in 1931

PART IV

The Prosecution and Trial of Elise and Roy

FIGHTING BACK

It didn't take long for Roy to fight back after the raid. Roy's lawyers threw the proverbial kitchen sink at the government's case, which the newspapers covered daily and in detail. In the months that followed the raid, Jerry Finch (Roy's lawyer and also a named co-conspirator in the case) brought numerous actions in an effort to disrupt the government case.

First, Finch wanted to keep the records seized in the raid from being presented to the grand jury or later at trial; second, Finch needed to prevent the wiretap transcripts from being given to the grand jury or being received in evidence at trial on constitutional grounds while undermining the integrity and reliability of how the transcripts were created; and third, Finch wanted to keep the government from seizing or destroying the radio station – it was a hard asset and Roy was going to need the cash from its sale or lease.

For Roy, there was a fourth and overriding concern – to protect Elise. That strategy involved painting her in the newspapers and in all public proceedings as detached from the bootleg business. She managed the radio station; she worked with Earl Gray's orchestra; she had her music and singing lessons; and she ran the household and soon would be a new mother.[165] There was no time for bootlegging!

The first article favorable to Elise and Roy appeared in the newspaper the day after the raid. The headline on the front page of The Seattle Star read: Aunt Vivien's Bedtime Tales Rudely Checked! Underneath it, a secondary heading stated: Mrs. Olmsted Hoped Radio Would Win Husband Respectable Place in Society.[166] The article began by introducing Elise to the reader and suggesting that she had been responsible, since their marriage, for persuading Roy to get out of the liquor business:

> *Few know Mrs. Olmsted. She is a London girl, a student, a musician and a vivacious, entertaining person. She has traveled extensively, studying her music in Italy. Somewhere, somehow, she met Roy Olmsted, declared to be the king of the Northwest liquor runners.*
>
> *Since their marriage Olmsted has been reported to have been more or less retiring from his former occupation. . . . [In the radio station Elise] saw the stepping stones on which her husband might make his way back into the respect of the community in which he lived. . . .*
>
> *Altho patient in her efforts to bring the station and her husband into the limelight of respectability, Mrs. Olmsted at times would flash fire at criticisms of Olmsted.[167]*

There is no way to know for certain that the story was planted by Roy and his lawyer Jerry Finch, but it certainly was timely and set the narrative for the legal maneuvering ahead. It also was an obvious exaggeration of Elise's history – traveling extensively, studying her music in Italy. There is no evidence that Elise in fact traveled anywhere outside of England before emigrating.[168]

More importantly, the story reveals two things about Elise that would be demonstrated time and again in the years ahead. First, she defended Roy vehemently throughout their marriage. Second, she believed she could reform him. And Roy seemed amenable to going straight as well, so this may have been a goal, if not a condition, of their marriage. In the end, she may have reformed him too much for their marriage to survive.

Roy next invited a newspaper photographer into the home in January 1925. The resulting photo collage appeared in the paper on January 15, 1925, just as the grand jury was receiving United States Attorney Revelle's evidence. It showed Roy, described as a "radio bug," sitting at "the broadcasting apparatus of his station KFQX" in their home. The other picture showed a smiling Roy and Elise in their kitchen on "cook's night out," with Elise wearing a chef's hat and apron, standing in the kitchen, cutting a slice of cake.[169]

This was all good coverage to win public opinion. But Roy was taking no chances, at least when it came to Elise's indictment. Roy resorted to what he knew best – paying bribes to get protection. He paid Assistant U.S. Attorney McKinney $6000 to keep Elise's name out of the indictment. Ultimately, it didn't work. Later, after the trial and with Roy now in jail, Elise bitterly admitted that a large sum had been paid to keep her "out of the picture." She said: "Roy paid plenty – they bled him dry then threw him down."[170]

Finch also painted Elise as a victim of rough treatment at the hands of Whitney and the agents conducting the raid. Within a week of the raid, on November 24th, Finch submitted affidavits from Elise, Roy and Al Hubbard, the boy inventor who Roy supported, to Judge Neterer, accusing Lyle, Whitney, and their agents of breaking the law by "willfully ëxceed[ing] their authority" and exercising it "with unnecessary severity."[171] Finch, unsuccessfully, asked the court to require the government to present the affidavits to the grand jury.

Elise's affidavit described the raid, the absence of any liquor found on the premises, the interference with her radio show, and she accused Whitney of assault in preventing her from calling the local police.[172] It is the first of several similar affidavits that Elise would provide in support of the motions brought by Finch.

Finch also filed a writ of certiorari with Judge Neterer, seeking the impoundment of the documents and records seized in the raid of his office several days after the raid on the Mount Baker home. Judge Neterer denied the writ and Finch filed an appeal to the U.S. Court of Appeals for the Ninth Circuit.[173] Among the documents seized by the agents during the raid was a quitclaim deed to the Mount Baker home from Roy to Elise, executed right after the raid on his home. Roy was hedging his bets in case he was convicted so that the house could not be seized as well, probably not imagining at this point that Elise could be charged, let alone tried in the conspiracy case.[174]

The next day, on November 25th, Finch went to state court on behalf of American Radio Telephone Company, the corporate entity through which Elise, Roy, and Hubbard owned the radio station, to obtain a temporary injunction against Lyle and Whitney, prohibiting them from damaging or destroying the radio equipment in Roy and Elise's home. Superior Court Judge William Gilliam entered a restraining order for Whitney and Lyle and ordered them to appear on December 3rd to show cause as to why the injunction should not be made permanent.[175] The complaint for injunctive relief stated that the station was purely a commercial venture, operating under a federal license and not engaged in any illegal activity. In what is perhaps the only statement that comes close to an outright denial that Elise's bedtime stories were coded messages, the Complaint denies any illegal use of the station and describes the bedtime story claim as "unjustly" made.[176]

Then on November 29th, Finch on his own behalf filed a lawsuit against Pacific Telephone & Telegraph Company for $31,000 in damages, alleging that the phone company allowed the wiretapping of his lines. The Superior Court set December 10th for a hearing on the petition to determine whether the phone company should be restrained from further allowing the wiretapping of Finch's lines.[177]

Al Hubbard, represented by Finch, also filed a lawsuit on December 11, 1924, against Immigration Commissioner Luther Weedin for $50,000, alleging false imprisonment the night of the raid in the detention station. Hubbard claimed he suffered "great pain and anguish of mind" from the arrest and had not been able to carry on his technical work as a result.[178] Hubbard was released without being charged.[179]

Finch next filed an application for an injunction before Judge Neterer in an effort to prevent the government from submitting to the grand jury documents and other materials seized during the raid from Roy's home and Finch's office. He also sought to prevent any wiretap evidence from being presented.[180] The grand jury was scheduled to meet on January 12, 1925, so the injunction plainly was designed to slow down or derail the government's case before the grand jury heard any evidence.

Judge Neterer denied the petition on January 8, 1925, and his opinion set the stage for what would come to be known as the "Whispering Wires" trial. He opined:

> *No authority has been cited, nor am I conscious of any which would destroy the competency of testimony based on conversations overheard while committing trespass upon property or franchise of another, and this includes, as presently advised, "wiretapping."*[181]

Undeterred, the same day on January 8th, Roy filed a federal lawsuit for damages against the agents involved in the November 17th raid. The complaint sought $31,000 in damages to his home and furnishings, including for the agents "spitting on the floor," for the cost of having to hire an attorney, and for mental anguish, loss of sleep, damage to his reputation and wrongful imprisonment for being forced to "associate with immoral and unclean persons" while in custody.[182] One can only chuckle at the brass of Roy's claims, but Elise had to be really angry at the damage to the house and her rough treatment.

For all the legal maneuvering, it had to be apparent to Elise and to Roy and his lawyers that the government had built a serious case and that it was going to go to trial. The government was confident that it finally had the evidence to shut Roy down and send him to prison. Prohibition Director Lyle made his case confidently in the newspapers repeatedly in the days that followed the raid:

> *Prohibition director Roy C. Lyle asserted positively yesterday that he has at last a complete chain of evidence that will put Roy Olmsted in the federal penitentiary. "I don't think it," said Lyle, "I know it."*[183]

"We regard the successful prosecution of Olmsted as the necessary first step toward annihilating the largest and most powerful rum ring with which the government has had to contend in the Pacific Northwest," said Director Lyle today… The efforts of the entire Prohibition enforcement force here are being concentrated upon this case."[184]

The Grand Jury Speaks – the Steady March to Trial

The grand jury met on January 12, 1925, and the outcome was never in doubt. It wrapped up its consideration of the evidence at the end of January with the indictment of Roy, Elise and 88 others for conspiracy to violate the Volstead Act. To add insult to injury, the grand jury, in a secret resolution, commended Director Lyle and his Prohibition agents for their diligence in conducting the investigation.[185]

Small victories. On February 18, 1925, in a separate hearing before Judge Neterer, charges for the possession and sale of liquor stemming from the November raid were dismissed against Roy, Elise and nine others arrested that night because the government found no alcohol during the raid.[186] The conspiracy charges, however, remained.

On April 6th, Roy, Elise, Finch on behalf of himself and thirty of the other defendants entered a plea in abatement[187] in Judge Neterer's court.[188] There were three reasons that Finch put forward to dismiss the indictment. First, the indictment was based on wiretap evidence and for the first time the troubling details of how the wiretaps were conducted were set forth. Finch had obtained several typed pages of conversation from an unnamed source to illustrate his point.[189]

Finch made the case that the conversations were not verbatim or actually recorded at all. They were overheard by agents who scribbled notes, which were then edited by Whitney's wife and edited again by Whitney and then neatly typed by Mrs. Whitney. When the agents didn't recognize the voice on the line, Mrs. Whitney provided the name based on her assessment of the context. The original scribbles were then destroyed. Worse still, Whitney did not let the grand jurors see the pages, but rather read selected conversations to them. Finch claimed these were doctored and unreliable, and he most certainly was right about that.

Next, Finch argued that Whitney had threatened the foreman of the grand jury to ensure an indictment was returned. Whitney had prepared a list of names of those the government thought should be indicted. He called the foreman out of the jury room and told him that he was caught on a wiretap as a customer of Roy's. Within two hours, the jury returned an indictment with Whitney's list of names filled in.

Lastly, Finch claimed the search of Roy and Elise's home was illegal because the agents had not found any alcohol but instead went on a "fishing expedition" to seize anything that would aid their case. Only on this ground would Finch make progress later in the proceedings.

Revelle of course moved to strike the plea in abatement. Judge Neterer heard arguments and then, two weeks later, he granted the government's motion. He decided that it was not his province to investigate the nature of the evidence relied upon by the grand jury. Nor was he concerned by the allegations against the foreman because a majority of the jury voted the indictment out and the foreman was only one vote.[190]

Undeterred, the defendants filed numerous motions to dismiss, for a bill of particulars or in demurrer. Judge Neterer ruled against the defendants in each case, finding that the indictments contained every element of the offenses listed and sufficiently apprised the defendants of the charges. On May 25, 1925, Roy, Elise, Finch and the others appeared in court to enter their pleas of not guilty.

One of the defendants, however, pleaded guilty, and it was a blow to the defendants. John McClean, Roy's chief dispatcher who took phone orders and arranged deliveries, pleaded guilty in exchange for a promise not to prosecute him. McClean's defection all but sealed the fate of Roy and his co-conspirators – he knew all the organizational details and would be the lead off witness for the government at trial.

As the summer progressed, Finch filed another motion to prevent the government from using the documents seized during the raid and to do the same with the wiretap evidence. On September 21, 1925, Judge Neterer granted the motion in regard to the seizure of the records and papers during the raid because the warrant was limited to seizure of bottles of illegal liquor of which none was found. It was a much needed but very minor victory for the defense.

As to the wiretapping claim, Judge Neterer had already tipped his hand in response to Finch's earlier motion to preclude the evidence being presented to the grand jury. The government's opposition to the motion revealed the true extent of the wiretapping and was shocking. The government had collected 1,560 transcript pages of conversations, neatly typed in three volumes. The lines to Roy's home had been tapped from July to November 1924.[191]

Still, Judge Neterer denied the motion, again finding that "[w]iretapping is not a national offense, nor made so by the statutes of the state of Washington; even so, it would not violate any constitutional right of the defendants to receive the testimony."[192] Finch and the defense were not done with their objections to the wiretapping and how the evidence would come in at trial remained to be decided. The issue would cause the most fireworks at trial.

Business As Usual

There is no doubt that Roy was under assault from all directions. Besides the grand jury, indictment and the government's methodical march to trial, the British Columbia authorities were looking into Western Freighters, Roy's British Columbia export company, now that they understood they were being cheated out of the $20 per case export tax. The Internal Revenue Service was also looking into Roy's bank accounts and the accounts held for him by others or under pseudonyms.[193] And Roy's entire organization had been rolled up for indictment, soon to be followed by Roy's customers if Revelle and Lyle were to be believed.

The other immediate result of the raid and subsequent legal proceedings was the disruption of Roy's cash flow. His personal life and business operations required a significant amount of cash to keep afloat. Now the new reality began to set in. The raid on the Olmsted home was not just a nuisance action aimed at harassing Roy. It was the capstone of a concerted investigation over the prior months and encompassed the entire Pacific coast trade.[194] The case was not going to go away any time soon. Roy's cash flow dwindled. His legal fees mounted and, without his well-oiled machine running, he couldn't get booze out of Canada or ensure bribes were paid in Washington to protect his shipments.

The irony of all of it was that Prohibition avoidance actually got worse in the wake of Roy being sidelined:

> *An immediate result of the "Olmsted" raid, federal prohibition agents charged today, had been the increased activity of the so-called "independent" bootleggers operating in Seattle. Virtually every type of boat used in rum running has been hurried down the Sound for a cargo of liquor for the Thanksgiving holiday trade.[195]*

It didn't take Roy long to realize that he needed to get back into the game to survive. In the Spring of 1925, he went back into business with Ed Engdahl, a former partner. Roy would handle the sourcing of alcohol in Canada and Engdahl would handle the landings and deliveries.[196] Roy turned to Hubbard to handle the financial dealings.

Hubbard soon learned to play both sides of the deal. The lure of easy money was too much and Hubbard was financially strapped. His wife had filed for divorce, which would mean alimony and child support, and his home-built radio business was faltering. He even moved back into the Olmsted home to save money while at the same time, in the consummate act of disloyalty, he was negotiating his informant's deal with Whitney.[197]

Whitney was able to get Hubbard hired as an agent, not just an informer, and in turn, Hubbard dropped his false arrest suit stemming from the raid and Revelle removed him from the conspiracy indictment. Hubbard was only 22 years old when in October 1925, he was formally hired as a Prohibition agent.

In November 1925, Hubbard was caught up in an arrest on Whidbey Island, salvaging a load of whiskey from the *Estrella*, which the Coast Guard had sunk the night before as a rum runner. Hubbard called Whitney who told him to not disclose his position. Then Hubbard called Roy to get the money to be bailed out. Roy was able to bribe the sheriff to get the charges dropped.[198]

Then, on the day before Thanksgiving, Whitney got a tip that a boatload of liquor would be arriving at Woodmont Beach south of Seattle. Sure enough, at 3 a.m., the boat arrived, offloaded and the agents sprang their trap. To their surprise, they caught Roy and Hubbard along with a deputy sheriff, three Japanese helpers and two more bootleggers the next morning, six cars, and 111 sacks of liquor.

The day after Thanksgiving, Whitney filed charges of conspiracy against the deputy, Roy, Hubbard and six others. Roy's smiling face was again on the front page of the newspaper.[199] Whitney told the papers that this was the first time Roy had been caught handling liquor directly since he had been dismissed from the police force years before:

> *In his palmy days he never touched a load; just directed his subordinates. He evidently was forced to do the actual work because of many recent reverses which have hit his pocketbook pretty hard.*[200]

Whitney was not far from the truth in regard to the financial impact of the bust. Elise raised the bail money and Roy was released the next day, only to be rearrested the next day by the Sheriff whose deputy had been caught. The Sheriff claimed that the deputy was in the process of arresting Roy's crew when the federal officers conducted their raid. The state case was a misdemeanor. Elise again had to come up with bail for Roy.[201]

With the original conspiracy trial scheduled to start in January 1926, the Woodmont Beach case would have to wait. In the meantime, Roy continued importing liquor but changed his base of operations to Whidbey Island. Finch continued to file legal motions and this time sought to have Roy tried separately, a motion that would be denied. The stage was now set for trial.

The "Whispering Wires" Trial – Prosecution First

The first day of the "Whispering Wires"[202] trial was Tuesday, January 19, 1926, but spectators hoping to get a seat began lining up outside the courthouse first thing Monday morning. It was pouring rain, a typical Seattle January day. The trial was high drama and entertainment in Seattle, and it would not disappoint. The newspapers made sure of that.

The courtroom was packed with the forty-six defendants and their lawyers, newspaper reporters, privileged spectators like Roy's elderly mother, and even law students from University of Washington. Few spectators could get a seat inside, but that didn't stop people of all kinds from coming to catch a glimpse of the participants.

There was a theatrical, dramatic atmosphere as the largest case of its kind ever tried on the Pacific Coast began. Curious-looking characters, some of them slovenly dressed and wearing dented derbies, others almost garishly attired, gathered in the hallway outside to scan the arriving principals.[203]

The story, therefore, by necessity, would have to unfold for the general public in the newspapers.[204]

The bailiff told the courtroom to rise for Judge Neterer, and as if on cue, Elise and Roy walked through the courtroom's door at the same time. The king and queen of the bootleggers had arrived, upstaging the judge. Elise and Roy walked to the front row reserved for them among the assembled defendants and took their seats.[205]

Roy was 39 years old at this point, Elise just 26. He was dressed to the nines in a dark suit with a derby hat. Elise likewise was the epitome of style in her modern cut suit of midnight blue with a brown fur collar – the "Woman in Blue" one correspondent dubbed her.[206] There was nothing humble about them. They did not appear chastened by the indictment or trial. They projected an air of amusement and nonchalance, as Elise whispered loud enough for some reporters to take note: "If you ask me, I think it's all a lot of blarney."[207]

Roy had been in and out of courtrooms enough to know what it was all about, first as a police officer testifying and then since his own troubles started in 1920. But the courtroom was all new to Elise. Anyone who has been through a trial, let alone a criminal trial, can appreciate the level of anxiety that Elise must have been experiencing notwithstanding her cool exterior.

The trial was not just a threat to Elise and Roy's livelihood, way of life and earthly possessions, but also to their very freedom. And for Elise, who was not a U.S. citizen, if convicted, she could be deported back to Canada or England. They had been living with the strain of anticipation of trial for over a year. And now on that first day of court, it seemed the plan was to project a high degree of insouciance and confidence in winning.[208]

As the day went on, the atmosphere changed. The newspapers could see that the government had organized a serious case and that the defendants were in for a fight. Elise and Roy's lawyer, Jerry Finch, himself a defendant, sought to have Elise dismissed from the case on the grounds that the government's wiretapping of the Olmsted home violated her privacy rights:

> *An eleventh hour desperate attempt to free Mrs. Elsie Olmsted, wife of former Police Lieutenant Roy Olmsted, from the toils of the government in the prosecution of the famous Olmsted liquor conspiracy case was made in federal court yesterday by Defense Attorney Jerry L. Finch. It failed.*[209]

The court decided that the wiretapping was legal and denied all the other motions brought by Finch.[210] Disappointment was beginning to set in as the jury was empaneled. Then came the government's opening statement by U.S. Attorney Tom Revelle. The Seattle Post-Intelligencer said it best:

> *All the fun, all the smiles, all the carefree jauntiness, all the joy of life, apparently, for forty-two defendants, suddenly fled the Olmsted trial yesterday when District Attorney [sic] T. P. Revelle opened the*

government's bag of accusations, and, for the first time, showed just what he had in it.[211]

Revelle had been a Methodist minister for 6 years before going to law school. He was fond of quoting the bible and his manner of public speaking was as if giving a sermon. He began by reading the names of each of the forty-six defendants and the four counts of the indictment – two counts of violating the National Prohibition Act by conspiring to unlawfully import, transport and possess liquor and to sell it, and two counts of violating the Tariff Act by smuggling alcohol into the U.S.[212]

Revelle outlined the breathtaking scope of the conspiracy in his opening statement, putting the defendants into two categories. The first group were the exporters, importers, and smugglers with their vast network of boats and landing spots throughout the coast. Then "there were the importers, like Olmsted and his wife… They reached into Canada and brought the liquor down in these speedboats operated by such men as Graignic… and others."[213] And he put Roy at the center of it all. One reporter summarized it this way: "Seattle [was] a vast liquor barony, with Roy Olmsted as its feudal lord and county and city law enforcement officials his personal henchmen."[214]

Of course, reading off Elise's name as a defendant in his opening, or identifying her as Roy's wife when naming the list of importers, is meaningless without specifically identifying what evidence the government intended to adduce at trial against her. But there were no specifics as to Elise and hardly a mention otherwise. Revelle made only one gratuitous swipe at her character: "In 1922, Elsie Olmsted attached herself to Roy and later married him. She kept his books and later assisted him."[215] In response, Elise "thrust out her little chin defiantly and glared level eyed at Revelle."[216]

What exactly did Revelle mean by "attached herself to Roy" in 1922? Remember, she was an informant for the government for at least the first half of 1922. She had to fear what was to come next given the government's accusations after the raid on the Olmsted home a year earlier. But the worst didn't come. There was no mention of her time as an informant for the government or questions about her former marital status, abandoning a child in Canada or illegally entering the United States through Washington.

Perhaps it is obvious but repeating those prior accusations also would have drawn objections from the defense and been improper in an opening statement as outside the time period of the indictment, even if the government had some evidence at the time that the accusations were true. As it is, the newspapers did not report any objection by Finch during the opening to Revelle's "attached herself" statement.

Later in trial, Whitney testified to meeting Elise in June 1922 as "Mrs. Potter," stating that she provided information on various shipments and gave Lyle the keys to Roy's safety deposit box.[217] The defense vehemently objected on the grounds that the conversation occurred over a year before the period covered in the indictment. The defense actually offered to prove that Elise had been an informant in the regular employ of the Prohibition office. Judge Neterer allowed Whitney's testimony, but later, during the defense case, he reversed himself and struck the testimony from the record on those very grounds.[218]

The government laid out its case against Roy and the others through its first witness – John McLean, Roy's dispatcher, who pleaded guilty in return for not being prosecuted. Roy listened impassively with his arms folded across his chest and McLean testified about the operation of the telephone exchange in the Henry Building in Seattle, the caches of liquor around town and the raids, and how Roy used a remote ranch – the Viele Ranch south of Seattle – as a staging warehouse for the liquor. Liquor transactions brought in a staggering $174,000 gross a month![219] The testimony was damning, and no one was left in doubt about the breadth of Roy's illegal operations.

The next witness was Peter Miller, the landscaper and gardener at the Mount Baker house. The government asked Miller to identify "Mrs. Potter." Remember that Roy and Elise introduced themselves in the neighborhood as Mr. and Mrs. Potter before they were married. Miller stepped down and walked straight to Elise's chair, extended his hand and tapped her shoulder as she visibly recoiled from him. Then she blushed.[220] The theatrical identification must have brought home the reality of the risk to Elise's freedom. It could not have been a good feeling.

This was not a prosecution tactic, however. Judge Neterer required each witness who was called upon to identify a person to step down from the witness box and go to the person rather than to say, "he's over there." Neterer's instruction was to "step down and go over and put your hand on his head."[221] No doubt, Judge Neterer did not think about the effect on Elise as the only woman on trial with the other men, but it was noticeable and palpable, and probably garnered some sympathy with the jurors, all men.

Revelle also used Miller to support his "unconventional relationship" comment in his opening statement, referring to the fact that Elise and Roy lived together in the Mount Baker home prior to their marriage. Vandeveer was on his feet objecting to the insinuations and improper testimony. Judge Neterer agreed and barred the government from making those remarks or eliciting such testimony or "ante-nuptial hints."[222]

By the end of the first week of trial, Roy admitted to reporters that he was feeling a little rough.[223] Almost all the evidence that first week had been directed against Roy and his role in the conspiracy. But Roy's loss was Elise's gain. Even the newspapers recognized that the only evidence against Elise was that "she once discharged a gardener, Peter Miller, because some beer had been missed from the garage."[224]

Roy tried to put on a good face. He posed for a photograph on the courthouse steps, wearing his derby hat, and standing with his mother and Elise before departing for the day. Asked about the trial, he said "Everybody's happy, aren't they? The government's having a good time. These are days of real sport."[225]

Then the government produced a surprise witness – this one aimed squarely at Elise. Mrs. Ruth Elbro, the wife of Roy's bookkeeper, Dick Elbro, and the former friend of Elise, voluntarily came from Vancouver to testify for the government. Dick Elbro had been indicted as part of the conspiracy, but he was not among the defendants at trial because he fled the jurisdiction to Vancouver.

Dick Elbro and Ruth Haughawout (her maiden name before marrying Dick) were witnesses at Elise and Roy's wedding. Ruth was a glamour girl who liked the high life. She became friends with Elise in the Fall of 1923[226] and later moved into the Mount Baker home with Elise and Roy. She was residing there in June 1924 with Roy and Elise until some time before they married.[227] A full-length photo of Ruth in the house is signed "Yours until the last apple falls."[228] The last apple apparently had fallen once Ruth's husband was indicted.

Ruth testified that she had "voluntarily" come to testify from Vancouver. The defense objected to her appearance and testimony, arguing that her testimony "violated every rule and policy of the law, especially because her husband is a defendant."[229] It was to no avail as Judge Neterer allowed the testimony. The defense was right. Ruth may have voluntarily testified, but she was bound by the marital privilege and the right to waive it belonged to her defendant husband, not her, but likewise, nothing prevented her from testifying against other defendants like Elise.

Revelle asked her if she knew Roy by any other name. "Yes," she said: "When I was introduced to him, it was by the name of Cosgrove. I also knew him as Potter." She testified that she also had met a dozen of the defendants as they "frequently conferred at Olmsted's residence at 3757 Ridgeway Place when she was there, which was several times a week during 1924." She said "[t]hey talked by themselves in the office on the second floor. Roy was in there, too, of course"[230]

Ruth also testified that the main defendants would meet at her house on Queen Anne Hill to confer as well. The house was used at one time as an office for the defendants.

Revelle asked her when Dick told her that he was working for Roy. Again, the question should have drawn an objection as the testimony was subject to the marital privilege, and it was hearsay besides. Ruth responded "[w]hen I first met him in November 1922." She added that Dick "was not keeping books for Roy at that time. He was driving a truck."

The government then asked Ruth about what Elise knew about the bootlegging:

> *Revelle: "What did Elsie say about the relationship between Trotsky and the others I have mentioned?"*
>
> *Ruth: "She said they were bootleggers – Roy's men."*
>
> *Revelle: "Did she say what she did?*
>
> *Ruth "No." ....*
>
> *Revelle: "What did Mrs. Olmsted ever say to you over the telephone about a houseboat on Lake Union?"*
>
> *Ruth: "She wanted me to rent such a houseboat, live in it and use the rest of it for a liquor cache. I refused, telling her I didn't want to be mixed up with liquor that way."*

Wrapping up, Ruth testified that she and Elise were "not the friends we used to be," perhaps the biggest understatement of the trial. The papers reported that Elise, wearing a gray fur coat and a small black hat "smiled as Mrs. Elbro testified," but that Mrs. Elbro "ignored her."[231]

Now it was the defense's turn. Ruth admitted that she knew that she could not be compelled to respond to the government subpoena from Vancouver, B.C., where she was then living. But, she added, looking directly at the defense counsel, that she "thought she should, wouldn't you?" "Not me," he replied, and then asked, "are you and Elsie still friends?" "Not exactly," she replied. Then, "[i]s there any enmity?" "Oh no, I just love her" with the emphasis on the word "love." "Was it because of that 'love' that you came here to testify?" The court sustained an objection to the question before Ruth could answer, but the point was made to the jury that she hated Elise.

And then the defense got to what must have been obvious to the jury – that there was some deal between the Elbro's and the government to obtain Ruth's testimony in return for not prosecuting Dick. "How many times did Mr. Revelle go to Vancouver to talk to you about this case?" Ruth's too-clever-by-half response was that she didn't "know that he ever went to Vancouver for that purpose, but once when he was there about six or eight weeks ago, I talked to him about it."

Ruth's testimony, if believed, could have been very damaging as it showed that Elise both had knowledge of the conspiracy and its members and also participated to some degree in its operation. But the jury must have viewed the testimony with the skepticism that it deserved. For example, Ruth's stated desire not to get mixed up in the liquor business by renting a houseboat to store it (if that telephone call truly ever happened) apparently didn't keep her from dating, living with, and marrying Roy's driver and bookkeeper over the prior two years.

As an aside, we don't know if there ever was an agreement between Revelle and either Elbro in regard to immunity or non-prosecution for testimony. It would have to be disclosed to the defense today, of course, but disclosure of potential impeachment evidence to the defense was not an established principle in the 1920s. Still, one wonders why Finch didn't ask more questions about whether the government made any promises in exchange for the testimony. More likely, Finch felt that Ruth's testimony was incredible and easily rebutted by Elise in her upcoming testimony. Why ask the question if you don't know the answer and give the opportunity to the government to validate the conspiracy further?

After Ruth came the government's "whispering wires" testimony. As a result of conversations overheard on the wiretap of the office phone on July 12th, Whitney testified the raids that followed deprived Roy and his organization of a month's worth of income.[232] Whitney also learned that day that Roy learned about the wiretapping.[233]

Wiretapping as a means of obtaining evidence had already been the subject of numerous failed defense motions on constitutional grounds. Now, at trial, the government still needed to get the specific evidence of each conversation before the jury, and that had to be done through the testimony of the listening agents. The wiretap "book" of compiled transcripts could not independently be admitted, and the defense objected to and exploited the testifying agents' lack of specific memory about any conversations.

Ultimately, the court ruled that the book could only be used to refresh a witness' recollection rather than be read into the record. And the agent hearing the conversation had to be the witness. The defense was not satisfied of course, especially because the court would not order that the defense be provided with a copy of the book.[234]

So the trial went on with more government agents testifying with "refreshed recollections." For context, Whitney, in his testimony, covered 216 conversations overheard while intermittently listening for a total of 26 hours and 24 minutes between 4:36 pm, July 8th to 7:35 pm, July 12th. It took him seven and a half court hours to deliver the testimony, and yet he estimated that he only provided a third of all the conversations that his agents will cover in their testimony.[235] For the next two weeks, the court and the jury, and those defendants in court, would hear conversation after conversation about the transport, distribution, and sale of liquor imported from Canada by Roy's organization.

While the sheer volume of calls buried Roy, the lack of any wiretap evidence involving Elise likely had the opposite effect. One agent (Fryant) testified that on July 5th, a woman telephoned the Henry Building office and said: "This is Elsie. Take a case of good stuff to the Fortune Transfer company." Vandeveer was on his feet with an objection because Fryant had not identified the speaker as Elsie, as in the defendant. Judge Neterer agreed and the testimony was stricken.[236] The government did not ask Fryant whether he knew Elise's voice or her recognizable English accent. It was perhaps a narrow escape for Elise.

Elise also was recorded on the home phone on August 16th. Another agent (Corwin) testified as to her exchange with Roy:

Elise: Did you call me?

Roy: Yes, I need some money… You've got a check with you, come down to Jerry's office. I've got an important date and can't leave.

Elise: Who's the date with?

Roy: I can't tell you.

Elise: I can't come down then.

Roy: Come on down.

Elise: If I come down, will you tell me?

Roy: Yes.

Elise: Alright.[237]

The newspaper found it humorous that even Roy had to ask his wife for a little money when he needed it, but it was the paper's additional observation that inadvertently captured Elise's character: "it disclosed a consuming curiosity on her part to find out with whom Olmsted had an important engagement."[238]

There were only a few innocuous and even humorous calls involving Elise. One reported wiretap conversation of Elise concerned a call with McLean about Roy being late for dinner. "You can tell him to go to hell," she reportedly said to McLean who responded: "That means, I guess, that he can get his pork chops downtown?" When the conversation was read in court, Elise apparently laughed, but not Roy.[239] She was captured again on October 21, 1924, answering phone calls at her home asking for Roy. She responded that he "had made a hurried trip to Vancouver and would be back the next day."[240]

There may not be many wiretaps of Elise because when she discovered the home phone was tapped, she had the telephone company install a new line with an unlisted number.[241] Regardless, by proving through extensive testimony that Roy ran the show, the government unintentionally but necessarily marginalized any involvement by Elise.

There was plenty to keep the newspapers and jurors interested in the trial as it wore on. But Elise appeared uninterested. Here's what one newspaper noticed:

> *Almost every principal in the Olmsted liquor conspiracy case exhibits constant interest in other people's business. It's part of the lawyers' business, most of the prisoners have a natural curiosity and the judge and jury are forced to pry into things.*

> *But Mrs. Elsie Olmsted, wife of Seattle's alleged bootleg king, is a shining exception.*

> *As one of forty-two defendants in the case, she attends every session of court — but always she attends strictly to her own knitting.*

> *And that can be taken literally as well as figuratively. Because she is always occupied with the manufacture of dainty beaded bags…. "I love to make beaded bags," she explained yesterday, "and I make so many that I couldn't possibly use them all myself. So I let my friends know that I'll make bags for them, provided they furnish the material. I've made fifty in the last year."[242]*

As the government case wound down, one last bit of evidence against Elise was brought in by the postmaster, Albert McLaughlin. He testified that PO Box 267 was registered in the name of Elsie Campbell. Roy had directed one of the Vancouver liquor houses to direct his mail to that address.[243] Of course, it had already been established in the trial that Elise went by the name Elsie Campbell when she entered the country and that Roy directed mail there says nothing about Elise knowing anything about it.

On the last day of its case on February 9th, the government moved to dismiss charges against ten of the defendants based on Judge Neterer's earlier ruling that evidence of purchasing liquor, even in case lots, was not evidence of conspiracy.[244] In all, seventeen of the defendants, including five who had pleaded guilty, were exonerated and freed.[245] The government concluded its case after eighteen actual days of trial.

The next morning, the court heard arguments on Finch's motion to dismiss Elise. Judge Neterer denied the motion: "No, that is a matter for the jury to decide."[246] It seems the improbable testimony of Ruth Elbro, Elise's former friend, of Ruth's alleged conversation with Elise about hiding a cache of liquor on a houseboat that Ruth should rent was enough evidence to keep Elise in the case.

The Defense's Turn

Now it finally was the defense's turn to speak directly to the jury. Finch, himself a defendant, and counsel for Roy and Elise, delivered the opening statement on February 10, 1926. As might be expected, Finch focused on the unreliability of the wiretap evidence, calling it "padded to suit this case."[247] He was right to a large extent, but in the aggregate, the volume of calls involving Roy, whose voice was clear to the agents listening, demonstrated the existence of a conspiracy even if many of the individual wiretaps were misattributed to others.

Conversely, Finch should have pointed out that there was an absence of any incriminating wiretap evidence against Elise. That fact would have made an impression on the jury had it been emphasized overtly. Addressing Elise in his opening statement, he told the jury:

> *So far as Mrs. Olmsted is concerned she is simply a housewife. She was pretty active in other things at the time. Besides the radio, she was interested in and taking singing lessons. She never had any connection with liquor interests and did not know anything about the room at 1025 Henry building.*
>
> *Mrs. Olmsted will tell you that at the time agents raided her house she and her family were at home entertaining guests, had just finished dinner, in fact. Earl Gray was there, and Foster the government radio inspector. Gray, you will remember, was leader of the Hotel Butler Cafe Orchestra....*
>
> *They were just putting on the customary bedtime stories over the radio, broadcasting with a radius of three or four thousand miles; these bedtime stories for the little kiddies. Mrs. Olmsted was doing this.*[248]

Finch finished by recounting how the raid was conducted, the absence of any liquor being found on the premises, calling people to bring liquor to entrap them, and then how Roy, Elise, and others were questioned and held in detention at police headquarters until 5 a.m., the next morning.

Finch's opening statement was risky in regard to Elise, stating that she never had any connection with liquor interests and had nothing to do with the liquor business. Risky, because Elise certainly knew everything from her days as an informant. None of the evidence about the operation of the liquor business heard during the government's case would have been a surprise to her. And all of that knowledge could have been used as impeachment once she testified. So it begs the question as to why the government didn't make use of her knowledge gained as an informant against her?

Elise's facade of innocence and lack of knowledge could have easily been pierced by bringing out her thorough knowledge of Roy's operations gained before they were married while she was an informant. It is true that the events took place before the period covered by the indictment, but that is no shield against impeachment of false or misleading testimony during trial. Finch's opening statement alone should have been enough to permit the impeachment of Elise. But it didn't happen. Instead, McKinney was courteous and deferential when he got to cross-examine Elise after her testimony.

Elise took the stand on February 11, 1926. Whether to testify as a defendant is not an easy decision, but here, Finch must have believed that she was capable of holding her own against the government prosecutors. She didn't disappoint. It was high drama.

> *Mrs. Elise Olmstead, wife of Roy, made her big move for freedom from the charge of conspiracy she faced in United States District Court, when she went on the witness stand yesterday afternoon and in her testimony cleared her skirts of any suggestion that she was engaged or aided in an illegal liquor business. . . . Whatever else may be said on behalf of Mrs. Olmsted in the trial, her own appearance on the stand, as a refutation that she is any rum queen or liquor partner, is the thing she will rely on for an acquittal.[249]*

She was mesmerizing:

She wore a blue, tailored suit, small, round blue hat and had a brown fur draped around her shoulders. Her girlishness was emphasized as she sat in the witness chair. During her testimony everything was smoothed on the surface but beneath it, particularly during cross examination was a subtle matching of wits, a steering clear of breakers and entanglements, yet she spoke frankly and without hesitation.[250]

Finch led Elise through his direct examination, first describing her busy life with music, working with Earl Gray and his orchestra to change the music from jazz to symphony, and then running the radio station. Then Elise testified about the raid, her rough treatment at the hands of Prohibition agents, and standing up to them bravely:

After the search was over and they found nothing, I regarded them as trespassers, but they hung around and wouldn't get out, so I started to call the police to have them put out and Mr. Whitney attempted to strike me in the face, in fact, he did push me against the wall.[251]

Elise next refuted the testimony of her former friend Ruth Elbro:

Finch: At any time did you have a conversation, like she said, in which you named various of the defendants as bootleggers?

Elise: No.

Finch: Did you ever propose, as she said, that she rent a houseboat, live in part of it and let the rest be used for a liquor cache?

Elise: No

Finch: Did you ever propose illegal liquor transactions to her?

Elise: I should say not![252]

Check. Finch should have sat down, having had Elise refute the only direct evidence offered against her. But inexplicably, Finch asked Elise about a "secret" phone:

Finch: Now, with reference to the tapped telephone, you knew that Beacon 4390, the regular line into your house, was tapped?

Elise: Yes.

Finch: What did you do about installing a secret phone?

Elise: About August 19, I had another telephone, Beacon 4790, put in. This was in addition to the regular phone. This new one at first was a party line, but in October it was changed to a one-party line, the number being Beacon 4981. We had it until Christmas.

Finch: Was it listed?

Elise: No.

Finch: Did you make arrangements not to have it listed?

Elise: Certainly. They had tapped the other and we didn't want this one tapped.

Finch: This secret phone was the one Mr. Whitney pulled away from you the night of the raid?

Elise: Yes, that was the first time he knew it was there.[253]

It is hard to understand what Finch thought he was accomplishing with questions about a secret phone. Elise had already testified that Whitney pulled "a" phone out of her hand so it made no difference which phone. Perhaps he expected McKinney to make much out of the fact that Elise had a secret, private phone from which she had the opportunity to take and make calls on Roy's behalf. It was dangerous territory made more so by Elise's statement that "we didn't want this [secret phone] tapped." Who was the "we" in that statement? Obviously Roy, but the government failed to pick up on it and point out to the jury how it looked to have kingpin Roy and his wife conspiring to install a private line to avoid government wiretaps on Roy's bootleg business.

Before finishing with Elise, Finch asked one last unnecessary question. He asked if Elise ever ordered a case of liquor to be sent to the Fortune Transfer Company. Recall that an agent had testified to overhearing a woman on the tapped home line named "Elsie" giving such instructions. The problem with the question was that Finch apparently forgot that Vandeveer had successfully objected to the testimony because the agents had not identified Elise as the woman on the phone.

Elise responded that she never even heard of the company until the day it was mentioned in trial. Yes, it was mentioned and then it was stricken from the record by Judge Neterer. All Finch accomplished was to unnecessarily remind the jury of the call answered by someone named Elsie at the Olmsted home.[254] And again, it is amazing that McKinney didn't ask his own agent whether the "Elsie" that took that call had an English accent!.

The cross-examination of Elise fell to McKinney, who would himself be indicted just four years later for taking bribes from Roy in exchange for information. Pausing for a moment, perhaps he went easy on Elise since he didn't uphold his part of the bargain in keeping

Elise out of the indictment. Or perhaps he had nothing in the way of evidence to use against her on the stand. We don't know. What can be said is that the cross-examination was ineffective, amateurish and poorly executed, with numerous missed opportunities. For example, McKinney could have asked her, since Finch re-introduced the subject of someone named "Elsie" answering the phone at the residence, whether there were any other women named Elsie in the home at the time of that call.

Instead, McKinney wasted his energy on largely irrelevant matters, for example, pointing out that Elise was off the air now – she was – and that she had no formal music training and did not graduate from any music conservancy – she didn't. Then he attempted to deflate the impact of the raid on her radio broadcast, referring to the agent who entered the studio:

> *McKinney: He didn't molest you?*
>
> *Elise: No*
>
> *McKinney: He didn't interfere with your broadcasting, did he?*
>
> *Elise: He most certainly did!*
>
> *McKinney: You were finished with the bedtime stories, weren't you?*
>
> *Elise: Yes, but I had to discontinue with the rest of the program.*[255]

It makes some sense that McKinney wanted to downplay the bad conduct alleged by Finch and others, but it really was not material to the government's conspiracy claim. It also makes some sense that McKinney didn't ask Elise whether her bedtime stories contained hidden messages, or, if she was aware that Roy used the radio equipment to communicate with his fleet of boats. She would have denied it all and the government had no proof otherwise.

Then McKinney shifted to the "secret" phone:

McKinney: And you knew the other line was tapped?

Elise: Yes.

McKinney: Why were you so solicitous that no one should hear what you said?

Elise: I didn't want my personal talks overheard any more than anyone else would. It was no one's business what I said over the phone.

McKinney: Was there any reason for you to guard your conversation?

Elise: Not necessarily, but it was private.

McKinney: Now the secret telephone number; you gave that to very few friends?

Elise: Yes.

McKinney: And as a rule, your outgoing calls went over that line, but most of the people who called, called on the other line, the one in the book?

Elise: No.

McKinney: You said only a very few had the secret telephone number. Suppose radio fans wanted to call in, they'd call on the phone that wasn't secret and so with other persons as a rule?

Elise: Yes.

Again, that Finch brought this entire subject of a "secret" number up in the first place is hard to understand. But then having been handed a gift, McKinney seems more interested in proving that the main home number that was tapped was the one used regularly by callers instead of getting Elise to answer tougher cross-examination questions such as admitting the secret phone was in the main hallway and Roy could have used it any time, as could anyone in the house, so many more orders could have been given and taken over that untapped line, especially since Roy knew the main number was tapped!

Having missed one opportunity, McKinney moved on to ask Elise about Miller, the gardener who had been discharged, and who pointed to Elise as Mrs. Potter, the "boss" who had him fired over the booze he found in the garage:

> *McKinney: [Miller was discharged] [o]ver some difficulty about intoxicating liquor?*
>
> *Elise: Oh, no, he was in the hospital with delirium tremens and we had to get another man.*
>
> *McKinney: He was just a sick man not able to work; there was no quarrel then?*
>
> *Elise: No.*

Elise again got the better of McKinney and explained away the last of the potentially damaging testimony from the government's case. Apparently, McKinney grew frustrated with Elise's responses and there was some argument between them, resulting in Judge Neterer admonishing McKinney not to argue with him once he ruled. Elise accused McKinney of trying to be facetious and later of being "all mixed up."[256]

Towards the end of his cross-examination, McKinney asked Elise whether the radio station had been installed in the mansion before she was married to Roy. It was. McKinney had asked Elise when she moved into the mansion. March 1924. Of course, she had not married Roy until August. The court sustained defense objections – again – to the government's clumsy attempts to inject Elise's alleged immorality into the trial.

The remainder of the defense case was taken up with further impeachment of the wiretapping evidence, and then the defense rested. Closing arguments took place on February 19th. Finch argued that this case was predicated on Whitney's hatred of Roy Olmsted and that the government would stoop to any level to get him. He said all of the government witnesses had been "paid" like McLean who got his freedom, and Ruth Elbro who testified so her husband could go free and come back to the U.S. But Finch saved his worst criticism for the government's treatment of Elise, as reported in the newspaper:

> *Mr. Finch flayed United States Attorney Thomas P. Revelle for what he terms the latter's cowardly insinuations against Elsie Olmsted at the opening of this case. These insinuations, he said, had not been made a part of the government's testimony but had been voiced merely for the purpose of prejudicing the jury against Mrs. Olmsted. Mrs. Olmsted, he said, should never have been brought into the case, and the only reason she was indicted was through the hatred of Whitney for Olmsted and anything dear to Olmsted.[257]*

After the final words were spoken by the lawyers, Judge Neterer gave his instructions to the jury. The instructions were published in full in the Seattle Daily Times on Saturday, February 20th while the jury continued its deliberations. Judge Neterer left little doubt that he believed the evidence proved beyond a reasonable doubt that Roy and some or all of the defendants had entered into a conspiracy. He also based his opinion on more than the wiretap evidence, upon which he instructed the jury to weigh the agents' testimony about what was said, their memory of it, and the identity of the speakers.[258]

But his instructions as to Elise's potential guilt could not have been more favorable to her:

> *Elise Olmsted [using her proper first name] in her own behalf denied any conversation attributed to her or any act attributed to her; denied that she asked Ruth Elbro, as testified to by Mrs. Elbro, to rent a house on Lake Union and use a part of it as an office and part of it for a liquor cache. You are instructed, that being the wife of Olmsted, if you should find that he was a party to the conspiracy charged, would not make her guilty of that conspiracy.*

> *She is accountable only for her own conduct and her own acts in conspiring or confederating with relation to the charge, and the mere fact that she is the wife of Olmsted or that she may have known that he was engaged in the unlawful enterprise charged would not of itself make her guilty.*

> *In my judgment, if she is connected with this conspiracy, it must be done by the testimony of Mrs. Elbro with relation to the conversation about renting a house for a liquor cache, and if her denial of that raises a reasonable doubt in your mind, then the doubt would be resolved in her favor, and she would be found not guilty.[259]*

Thus, in the judge's mind and as he so instructed the jury, the case against Elise came down to one thing: who do you believe, Ruth Elbro or Elsie Olmsted? All the rest of the evidence against Elise, meager as it was, was ignored by the court in its instructions.

The jury got the case late Friday, February 19th, after what must have seemed like a marathon thirty-two days of trial and 125 witnesses. They deliberated until midnight on Friday and returned the next morning for more. They went to lunch at noon and shortly after returning, announced that they were ready to deliver their verdict.

The courtroom was packed with those waiting to hear the verdict, government, defendants and spectators alike. The newspapers tried to capture the tension in the air, and noted that the jurors said not a word to each other, nor did they smile. A bad sign. The judge ordered the bailiff to read the verdict. Starting with Roy, the bailiff announced "guilty as charged" on the first count, followed by Jerry Finch as guilty, then policeman Reynolds, not guilty, and through the rest of the names on both counts. It was a nerve-wracking way to read the verdict.

Remarkably, the newspaper account recited the verdicts but somehow failed to report Elise's acquittal in the article! A photo of Elise and the others found "not guilty" at least accompanied the article.[260] Roy was philosophical as he posted his bond, saying he was satisfied with the verdict and that the jury did their duty as they saw it. Elise said: "That's what we expected as far as Roy and myself.[261] Roy was released on his bond pending an appeal. The trial was over. But the government wasn't yet done with Roy.

Word hit the newspapers that the government was ready to indict Roy again, this time for his part in the Woodmont Beach case arising from the Thanksgiving 1925 raid where Roy was caught with Al Hubbard landing booze. The case had been on hold pending the outcome of the Whispering Wires case.[262] The Woodmont Beach indictment was going to be the government's insurance that Roy would go to jail regardless of the outcome of his anticipated Whispering Wires appeal.[263] With the help of Hubbard, the government was putting together a much larger conspiracy case against Roy. It focused on the period after the raid on the mansion and was purported to include many government officials whom Roy had bribed along the way. Roy was about to face more trials, more expenses and perhaps more time in prison.

The Money Dries Up

As if the government's relentless enforcement actions against Roy weren't enough, that worker who had been injured by Roy's first wife in a car accident in 1921 mentioned earlier? He still had his unfulfilled judgment in hand. He filed a petition in superior court for a seizure order of Roy's personal property in satisfaction of the remaining $4000 unpaid debt on the judgment for damages.[264] Also, Treasury agents also showed up in court seeking orders to obtain bank records in their investigation of Roy's income, although they would be ultimately unsuccessful.[265]

Roy, in his efforts to raise money, was paying none of his bills. Their former gardener sued and won a judgment for $412 for unpaid services while Roy was selling the house.[266] Then there was Elise's nurse. She sued and won a judgment of $142 plus interest for services while Roy and Elise were absent during trial. Mary E. Roth, a trained nurse, had been retained November 11, 1925, through April 11, 1926, at the rate of $7 per day. She had received $914 and sued for the balance owed.[267]

Then there was Prosper Graignic, Roy's trusted and loyal boat captain who had jumped the bond Roy provided in the Whispering Wires case and was now a wanted man. Roy assisted the U.S. Marshal to arrest Prosper on April 2, 1926, on a steamship coming from Vancouver to Seattle. Worse, Roy actually drove the Marshal to Vancouver in his own car, arriving as the ship was ready to depart. Roy met with Prosper aboard the ship, and the arrest was made when they entered U.S. waters.[268]

Revelle said that Prosper had actually been prepared to plead guilty and tell all he knew about Roy's operations at the time of the trial, but he disappeared, no doubt at Roy's insistence. Now Roy's interest in the $4000 bond he had backed for Prosper made it more convenient for Prosper to return.[269]

With legal fees mounting and the cash flow dwindling from his operations, Roy was desperate for cash so he put the Mount Baker house on the market. Putting a brave face on it, Elise said that "we had the home up for sale long before the trial started. We just decided to sell – that's all. There's no need to sell, but we just thought we'd dispose of the place."[270]

When asked about their plans, Elise offered a rosy picture and a bright future:

What are our plans? Oh, Roy still has his radio business, you know. He sells radios and we still own the broadcasting station. Mr.

Olmsted has dropped the exporting and importing liquor business. I mean the business of shipping liquor from Canada to Mexico, of course.

I heard Roy talking over the telephone yesterday to some newspaper reporter. When the interview was published it had him declaring that he saw no crime in buying and selling booze. What he meant was that he thought it was no worse to sell liquor to people who wanted it than it was to buy it. What's sauce for the goose is sauce for the gander, if you get the idea."[271]

She wanted the reporter to know that they were making plans for the future, something she would be ready to announce in a week: "I think you'll be interested in knowing but we can't say a word now about it…. I can't even say now what the plans concern, further than they concern us."[272] Whatever it was on her mind did not materialize, and despite her brave face, the future was not bright. But again, this is classic Elise – an air of mystery to deal with a harsh reality.

The house sold quickly. The furniture came next. On March 16, 1926, a Notice of Auction appeared in the newspaper for the sale of their furniture and household effects: "Mr. and Mrs. Roy Olmsted have sold their beautiful home and have taken apartments, so they have commanded us to sell all that is left of their furniture after furnishing their apartments.[273] The auction was set for March 18th.[274]

The reporter covering the sale set the stage: "From the four corners of the world Mrs. Olmsted obtained the beautiful furnishings for her home, and now they are to be scattered again. In a few hours articles that cost thousands of dollars will be sold."[275] The newspaper reporter found her getting ready for the auction "dressed in a pretty striped morning dress, with a matching silk band holding in her bobbed locks… very much the housewife."[276]

Again with a brave face talking to the reporter, Elise asked herself the question out loud: "Do I hate to part with all these things?" She "shrugged her shoulders with gay indifference" and said:

> *Perhaps it will be better if we don't have so much, and besides we can get them again some time. Besides I'm keeping the furniture I need for my new home – my Persian rugs and my piano so I can go on with my music.*[277]

Elise declined to say where they were moving to because she wanted to keep the location secret so she could work on a book – a book about her experiences as "wife of a so-called bootlegg [sic] king."[278] She never wrote the book.

The government, however, knew where Elise and Roy moved. Their new house was at 1000 Shelby Street, up a block from the waters of Portage Bay in Seattle.[279] Just a few weeks after moving, Elise had quite a fright. In late May 1926, Elise was driving near her home when the car crashed. According to the police report, her car had been sabotaged. The bolts on the rear tires had been loosened.[280] No one was ever held responsible, but one wonders whether it was a joke gone bad or something worse.

The fact is that Whitney and the Prohibition agents were keeping Roy under tight surveillance. Fair enough. Roy was still in the business. Tensions were high and Roy apparently argued several times with agents Fletcher and Thompson who were doing the watching. The encounters escalated after several months, ending with

Roy getting bludgeoned with a blackjack, several shots being fired and ultimately Roy being arrested.[281]

In Roy's version of events, he spotted Fletcher watching him while he walked his dog one night (apparently Roy and Elise got a German Shepherd at some point). He went over to see Fletcher, kidded with him and then started to walk away. Roy said Thompson came running from behind the car and yelled he was under arrest, hitting him with the blackjack and drawing his revolver. Thompson shot twice at the dog but missed. Roy then said that Elise came out of the house, and he had to hold her back from tearing into Thompson and Fletcher.[282]

The agents' version was the opposite, saying that Roy had threatened Fletcher and when Roy went for him seated in the car, Thompson went to his assistance. Roy was taken to jail but released on $250 bail with the understanding that he was going to be charged with assaulting an agent. Roy responded that he was going to prefer charges for assault against Thomson, and Roy had the black eye to prove the assault.[283] Nothing apparently came of the incident, but the surveillance continued.

The surveillance, of course, was justified as Roy continued to bring booze into Seattle by various means, including hidden in railroad tankers. Hubbard was now reporting to Whitney regularly. By May, Whitney was ready to bring a second conspiracy case against Roy, covering his activities after the raid in November 1925 through May 1926. The case would be known as the Second Olmsted case.

Whitney charged a broader conspiracy against Roy and the dozens of other bootleggers in his organization as well as members of the corrupt police force.[284] The grand jury indictments came on May 13, 1926, and bench warrants for arrest of the defendants.[285] As many as 200 people had been named in the indictments. But Elise was not charged this time. Perhaps her prior acquittal was enough for Revelle and Whitney to avoid another sideshow with slim evidence. Or more probably, there continued to be no evidence of Elise's involvement in Roy's operations.

Roy turned himself in for arrest on the indictments, and he posted bond again to remain free. The indictments gave Whitney what he wanted though – more insurance against Roy walking free on the Whispering Wires conviction if Roy was successful in his appeals.

Just two days after the Olmsted indictments, The Seattle Star reported the sensational story that Al Hubbard had long been a Prohibition agent helping the government. Hubbard admitted it, saying: "I guess a lot of people will be trying to remember when they last saw me now that I have been identified as a Prohibition agent."[286] Elise refused to comment on Hubbard's betrayal: "For his wife's sake, I don't want to hurt Al. I can't hurt him without hurting her also and we're very good friends, as good now as we were before."

It is certainly true that a lot of the people were worried about Hubbard's betrayal – Seattle policemen, low-level government people and Coast Guard and Customs officials. A separate case had been brought against Officer Comstock and a handful of other allegedly corrupt policemen. Assistant U.S. Attorney Colvin used the opportunity to bring in and interview Roy and Elise – Roy was not charged in the Comstock case.

He and Elise were interviewed separately. We don't know what was said in those meetings, but a rumor spread quickly that Roy himself was working for the government. There is little doubt that the discussion was about trading Roy's information for leniency, something Elise had been in favor of all along. But the rumor was wishful thinking that Roy would testify voluntarily before the grand jury looking into graft charges against public officials thanks to Hubbard's information.[287]

Roy quickly quashed the story: "It's their show, and I am not interested. In fact, I would appreciate very much being left alone."[288] A reporter asked Roy whether Elise was going to testify. He replied: "Why, I haven't even discussed with my wife what was the result of her conference with Mr. Colvin."[289] The newspaper ran a photo of Elise stating that she was leaving her meeting with Assistant U.S. Attorney Colvin, having outlined "her knowledge of graft in city and county government."[290]

The next day, the newspapers reported that the government's key witness, Mark Fleming, had disappeared. He was dismissed from the Whispering Wires trial the prior year and was known as the "fixer" for any bootleggers arrested. Moreover, the newspapers reported that neither Roy nor Elise had agreed to testify before the grand jury.[291] So the government went back to building its graft case from scratch. The government had plenty of people to talk to about trading prison for testimony.

Prosper Graignic was one such person: "To an apparently growing list of defendants who may be expected to testify as government witnesses at pending liquor conspiracy trials in Federal

Court the name of Prosper L. Graignic, charged as a rum boat operator under four indictments, may be added."[292] Prosper, recall, was indicted in the Whispering Wires case but disappeared before he could be arrested, only to be arrested with the help of Roy after the trial. Out on bail, he was indicted in the Second Olmsted case, was arrested again but was released on his own recognizance – a sure sign that he was now cooperating as the government readied its cases for trial.

Adding to the government's momentum, the Ninth Circuit Court of Appeals upheld Roy's conviction on May 9, 1927, on a 2-1 vote.[293] While the majority found wiretapping to be constitutional, the dissenting judge made such a compelling case against wiretapping as an unwarranted search that it gave the defense hope the Supreme Court would take the case and reverse the conviction. Roy and the other defendants in the Whispering Wires trial filed a motion for rehearing in the Ninth Circuit, continuing the appeal.[294]

The Second Olmsted Trial and the Woodmont Beach Case

The Woodmont Beach case – the one where Roy was caught on the night before Thanksgiving landing liquor – was scheduled to be tried on June 6, 1927, but the government asked the court for a delay because a key witness was out of town. Judge Neterer put the trial over to a future date. Roy already was under $18,000 in bonds for his appeals and other charges and added $3,000 to it for the Woodmont Beach case.

The Second Olmsted Trial was now scheduled to begin on October 18, 1927. Seventy-seven men were indicted and fifty-one of them had been arrested and were expected at trial. But Roy was nowhere to be found on the eve of trial.[295] The newspapers asked: "where is Roy Olmsted, himself?"[296] Whitney was sure he had fled the jurisdiction before trial, but Elise denied it:

> *That's just propaganda the government officials are spreading, in my opinion. Roy will be there when the trial opens — unless someone shoots him or something. I think some of the officials have more to be afraid of than he has, from the way they talk.*[297]

Taken at face value, the quote reveals a few things. Elise may not have known where Roy was or if he would show up. She did not like being kept in the dark. And second, it became a recurring thing with Elise that she saw power and opportunity in Roy's knowledge about graft and corruption in the city — something that could be traded for Roy's freedom.

Roy did not appear. "The King is – Gone!" said the headline. He "vanish[ed] as mysteriously as his rum boats once lost themselves in the swirling night fogs when pursuit was close."[298]

A bench warrant was issued and his $3000 bond was forfeited. Proper Graignic also went missing. So much for the rumor that Prosper would testify in return for his freedom. Some of Roy's friends told reporters that Roy went to Canada because the exoneration of numerous other defendants rested on his absence from trial.[299] It was all speculation. Apparently, even Elise didn't know for sure.

The trial went forward without Roy. Hubbard was the star witness for the government. The case took only five days. Of the thirty-nine defendants, the jury convicted just fourteen - only the rum-runners. They acquitted all the public officers, deputy sheriffs, and Seattle policemen. And since the convicted defendants were the same bootleggers convicted in the Whispering Wires trial, the court ordered the sentences to run concurrently with their sentences in the first trial inasmuch as the conspiracy was a continuation of the conduct charge in the first case.

Elise agreed to a wide-ranging and poignant interview that appeared in the newspapers the day the trial started. The reporter who wrote the story was Marie Dunbar. She had studied journalism at the University of Washington and worked for various newspapers, covering legislative affairs. She was the perfect, empathetic voice to paint a sympathetic image of Elise – in Dunbar's mind perhaps, Elise was another woman done wrong by a cheating, fleeing husband abandoning his wife and baby. Dunbar was a single mother with a young child.

Dunbar had married John H. Dunbar who became the Attorney General for Washington in 1923. They had a daughter, Dorothy, in 1922, and two years later, Dunbar ran off with his secretary. Dunbar would go on to have a brilliant career as a society columnist and author – her life story is as remarkable and interesting as Elise's, but much more transparent and open.[300]

Dunbar's interview with Elise appears beneath this headline: "Silence is Mrs. Olmsted's Role." Above the headline is a collage of pictures of Elise and Roy and their home with the following description: *During the days of opulence, when the sun was shining on the Olmsteds in their Mount Baker home, Roy celebrated a birthday with a cake made by the fair Elise. But now "the cake's all dough," the home is sold, Roy is said to be broke – and a fugitive.*[301]

How Dunbar got this interview is unknown. Elise certainly had become adept at manipulating the media and getting sympathy for her situation. But it seems so unlikely that Roy would have left without telling Elise he was going, where he was going or for how long he would be gone. If he did slip away without telling her, it seems natural enough that she would be disappointed in him about it and would arrange the interview to tell him so. But it is just as likely that Roy and Elise used the interview to continue to paint Elise as separate from these legal troubles, insulating her against future actions. We just don't know for sure. You decide how genuine the article is after reading the interview:

Silence is Mrs. Olmstead's Role

> *Where shadowy forms slide through early morning dawn and booze basks in the joyfulness of romance and mystery shrouds it all, there stands one woman, a little dark-haired, dark-eyed person who looks somewhat like the fragile ladies carved on cameos, and she stands and talks, frankly, dispassionately, openly.*

> *She is Mrs. Elise Olmsted, wife of Roy Olmsted, one-time booze baron, convicted of conspiracy and missing defendant in the present federal court liquor trials.*

No Sudden Impulse

> *"I did tell the newspapers that I was certain Roy would be here for trial. I was certain he would. I spoke in good faith," commented Mrs. Olmsted as she sat in her apartment at the Blackstone, 322 Summit*

Avenue, yesterday. "But this matter of Roy not appearing for trial is not the result of a sudden impulse. I know that. There have been certain people talking to him. They have changed his mind."

Why, defendant after defendant has come to me and pledged themselves to pay Roy's bond if he stayed away. Now no one but a bootlegger would be dumb enough to figure that because a man had been convicted by the courts once he had no show to be cleared on another charge."[302]

And there Mrs. Olmsted sits and waits, and until recently she hoped – hoped that Roy would face trial – that's the story she whispers and hints of between the lines of her conversation – and be vindicated.

Doesn't Know

"I do not know where he is, and that is the truth," declares Mrs. Olmsted. "Of course, if I did, I would not tell, but I absolutely do not know where Roy is."

And then Mrs. Olmsted in her fascinating English accent talks of the Hubbards, courts, trials, bootleggers, music, her baby and –

While somethere Roy waits for the law to dim its vengeance, Mrs. Olmsted moves cheerily around her apartment, an apartment furnished with the remnants of her luxurious home – Oriental rugs, deep-cushioned chairs, fine soft-colored old tapestries – the home that they lived in out at Mount Baker Park before federal officers camped on their doorstep.

And while she waits she does not lose herself in bitterness. Mrs. Olmsted has a little two-and-a-half-year-old girl. She teaches the child German and French, being a linguist herself; she plays her piano – and she waits and waits.

But Mrs. Olmsted is not the type who would sit and weep over her husband's slippers he left behind him and drop tears on his overcoat that hangs in the family closet. No, indeed, Mrs. Olmsted is carrying on with her little girl.

"It is wonderful to have something to work for," she commented as she picked up the baby's dolls and books from the living room floor. "Oh, Roy — no I don't know when he will be home. Ask me another."

And it was hard to decide whether it was attempted gayety, contempt for the man who did not appear at trial, love of a sturdy rather than sentimental type, or just what that asserted itself in that laugh. At any rate, the laugh was a failure and it's easy to see that there is one person who is disappointed that Roy Olmsted did not show up in federal court yesterday.

That person is Elise Olmsted, his wife, who knows of booze smuggling ways dark and devious, but who talks in terms of open frankness and exquisite English.

Another week with more speculation passed when the newspapers reported on October 28th that Roy "has landed in Mexico. And has the situation well in hand."[303] Apparently, friends of Roy had received word from him that he intended to stay in Mexico to establish a new liquor import/export company. Elise was supposedly preparing quietly to join Roy in Mexico.[304] Others thought Roy had fled to Canada, but Elise told federal agents who continued to hunt for Roy that he was not in Canada as supposed. Instead, she told them, "[h]e's in hiding around here and will come out when he gets ready."[305]

Roy's other pending indictment – the Woodmont Beach case – was scheduled for trial on November 8, 1927. Apparently, Roy was ready to come out of hiding at the end of October because, to the surprise of the government, he surrendered and appeared in court knowing that he would be taken into custody and likely spend a night in jail unless and until a bond could be arranged. Jaunty as ever, Roy said, "I have made my reservations and expect to be a guest of Uncle Sam for some time."[306] Prosper Graignic, his trusted rum boat captain, also surrendered and was in custody pending a bond.

To a group gathered in the corridor outside the courtroom, Elise said "I have been Roy's custodian. Here he is. I told you he would come in when he was ready."[307] When asked where he was all this time, Roy said "Why, I was around here all the time. I would have to do some fast traveling to be all the places the reports had me."[308] Roy was not able to make bail at $10,000 and remained in the King County jail.

The Woodmont Beach trial commenced on November 15, 1927. Hubbard was the first government witness. He testified that he went to Roy's house the night before Thanksgiving and Roy told him that Engdahl had brought a load of liquor in. While driving to Woodmont Beach, he said, Roy told him that he wasn't worried about the landing because he had talked to Lee Parker, the deputy sheriff, to make sure it went alright. Parker, who was testifying under immunity, then took the stand to say that Roy had called him up the day before Thanksgiving to meet him at the landing.[309] Finally, Whitney testified that after the arrest, Roy admitted to him that he had been caught red-handed.[310] It seemed like an airtight case against Roy.

For the first time in any of the proceedings against him, Roy took the stand in his own defense. He disputed Hubbard's testimony, stating that the liquor belonged to Hubbard and he went along to the landing to help him unload it. Roy asserted that he knew Hubbard was a Prohibition agent at the time: "Hubbard had told me before this that he was a prohibition agent, and I know I did a foolish thing when I went out with him, over my wife's protest. But I was curious to find out just what his game was."[311]

Keep in mind the timeline here – Hubbard became a Prohibition agent in October 1925 after sharing information and negotiating with Whitney for two to three months. Roy was convicted in February 1926 in the Whispering Wires trial, but Hubbard was not a witness or disclosed as an informant in that trial. Roy later learned directly from Revelle and Whitney in May of that year that Hubbard in fact was a Prohibition agent; he certainly read The Seattle Star's sensational story as well. Yet here he was testifying that he knew about Hubbard prior to November 1925. Revelle pounced on the inconsistency: "You were at my house in May 1926. And you wanted to know if Hubbard was a Prohibition agent. You said you never knew it before and you threatened to tell the newspapers," Revelle thundered.[312]

In response, Roy said he was only seeking confirmation of what he already knew, and he then dropped a political bombshell:

> *You say I came out to your house to find out if Alfred M. Hubbard was really a prohibition agent, and although I did come out for that purpose, you have neglected to say that you promised me the pardon. You also told me I was a pretty good fellow, and you would do something for me. When I asked you what it would cost, you told me*

you wanted me to help you 'get' the officials. You promised me a Presidential pardon if I would help you 'get' certain city and county officials to whom I had been paying graft money.[313]

Roy said that he wasn't interested in the deal. He testified that he told Revelle that "[b]efore I'd complain about anybody else having a dirty backyard, I'd clean out my own."[314] The jurors must have been astonished by the breadth of duplicity, lies and graft of all parties, from Revelle and Whitney, to all the unnamed officials, to the law enforcement officers on the take, and to the bootleggers. How can one person alone be guilty when everyone is guilty?

But it may have been the testimony of Elise in the end that turned the tide. She took the stand at the end of the defense case and testified that Hubbard had come to the Olmsted house the night before Thanksgiving and gotten her husband out of bed to help him. She heard him ask Roy "to come down to Woodmont Beach to help him unload a cargo of his – Hubbard's – liquor." On cross-examination, she said she overheard the conversation which took place in the hallway outside their bedroom.[315] And, Roy assured her, it would be fine because Hubbard was a Prohibition agent.[316]

Roy was acquitted. Had Elise perjured herself in Roy's defense? Almost certainly. But the acquittal didn't buy Roy his freedom. He remained in jail pending trial in the Second Olmsted conspiracy case having forfeited his bond by disappearing on the eve of trial.

It is useful to pause for a minute in the legal proceedings to observe two things. First, Roy and Elise didn't have $10,000 in cash available to pay the bond. His cash flow had dried up and he was unable to secure the money. Second, none of his cohorts or political backers were interested in putting their money on the line for Roy, nor were bonding companies likely to do so with Roy's prior forfeiture history without substantial collateral, which he lacked. In short, Roy and Elise were broke and faced the prospect of Roy going to jail for four years and paying the $8000 fine from his first conviction.

And another pause is appropriate too. Remember that the Second Olmsted conspiracy case was tried in October without Roy because he skipped bail. The government only got convictions of the rum runners while the rest of the defendants were acquitted. And worst of all, the sentences of those convicted were to run concurrent with their sentences in the Whispering Wires trial. Still, Whitney and Revelle were content to hold Roy in jail as long as possible while they waited for the Supreme Court ultimately to decide Roy's fate. If the Court reversed, Revelle and Whitney hoped that they still could get a conviction in the second trial, which was not based on wiretap evidence but rather on Hubbard's testimony. It was a long shot. If Roy made bail before the Court acted, they were sure, in their minds anyway, he would to flee to Canada or elsewhere.

And it looked like their worst fears were going to come true because, somehow, the ever persistent and resourceful Elise raised the bail money. We don't know from whom, but Elise hurried to the Marshal's office to try to spring Roy. Unfortunately, it was too late. The same day, on November 21, 1927, the Supreme Court denied Roy's appeal:

> *On the verge of obtaining his freedom by posting $10,000 in bonds*
> *in the "second Olmsted conspiracy case," and jubilant over his victory*

of last week when a jury acquitted him of smuggling charges, the former Seattle police lieutenant received a blow today when the United States Supreme Court refused to review the "whispering wires" conspiracy case of last year in which Olmsted and twenty others were found guilty.[317]

Revelle was ready to ensure Roy didn't get the chance to flee. He refused to accept the bond and by the time Elise arrived with the surety, Revelle had already sought a commitment order from the court. There was no way that he was going to let Roy go free or slip away again now that the Supreme Court had ruled against him.

On the morning of November 29, 1927, Roy was told he was to serve his sentence on McNeil Island. Elise and Roy's little daughter, Patricia, now just over two years old, Roy's mother, father, and brothers, and a crowd of interested spectators gathered to see him off.[318] Unfortunately, there is no photograph to memorialize the larger scene.

One newspaper reporter asked, "what do you suppose Roy carried with him to prison?"[319] It was a portrait of Elise that she made for him. It was inscribed "Elise Olmsted in a fighting mood."[320] A picture of the framed portrait is shown above the newspaper article with the caption "A New Song of Love" and description: "Love has been sung in many keys and many themes, but Elise Olmsted possesses the love that fights and battles and never gives up."[321] Here again, we see the resolute Elise – her persistence in the face of adversity and her unwavering defense of Roy.

In Elise's own words, on a day that must have been one of the hardest of her young life – she was 27 – she told reporters, bitterly:

It is the picture he likes best of me – it's the one that expresses my attitude today. It's hard enough to fight when you are out, but – Well, I've learned a lot about the so-called brotherly and sisterly love. Perhaps a hard twisted version of it.

The other day I was walking along the street and a woman rushed up to me, a woman I had never seen before, whom I did not know, and said "I am a member of W.C.T.U. [Women's Christian Temperance Union]. I hope they get you! A Christian spirit? Hardly.

When I stop – well that's a long time off and you know a battle well fought – well anyway, I'm going to win. I know I am."[322]

It would be a longer fight than she thought it would be, but in the end, she would win for Roy.

A Short Stay in Prison

Despite last-minute efforts to stay the commitment, which ultimately failed, Roy was taken to McNeil Island to begin serving his sentence. Here is what he could expect on his first day according to the newspapers:

This morning he will be put "through the mill," and emerge a different person. His hair will be clipped close, he will be "mugged" and fingerprinted, and will don the garb of prison gray. And for the next few years Roy Olmsted will cease to exist as an entity - he has become "Number 6538."[323]

There were no resort prisons then. Inmates worked. As the warden put it: "We'll keep him working outside, at least until he gets the softness worked out of his system. We haven't any bartender's position open just now."[324]

A week later, Roy was sawing wood on the beach for the prison to use as firewood and told one of the officers that he was enjoying the hard work. He referred to himself as the "beachcomber of the pen."[325]

As Christmas approached, Roy wrote Elise two poems from his cell.[326] The poems appear on a yellow sheets of paper, side by side, below a hand-drawn Christmas scene by Roy.

A copy of the poems, which was saved by Elise, is reproduced here.

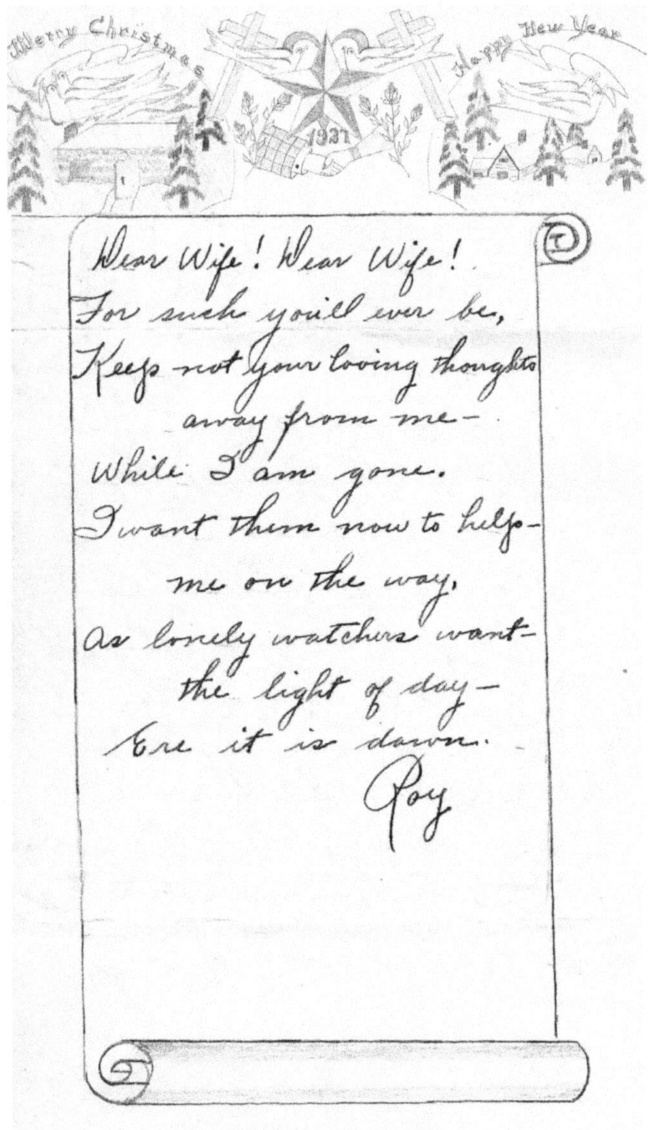

Roy's Christmas Poems to Elise 1927

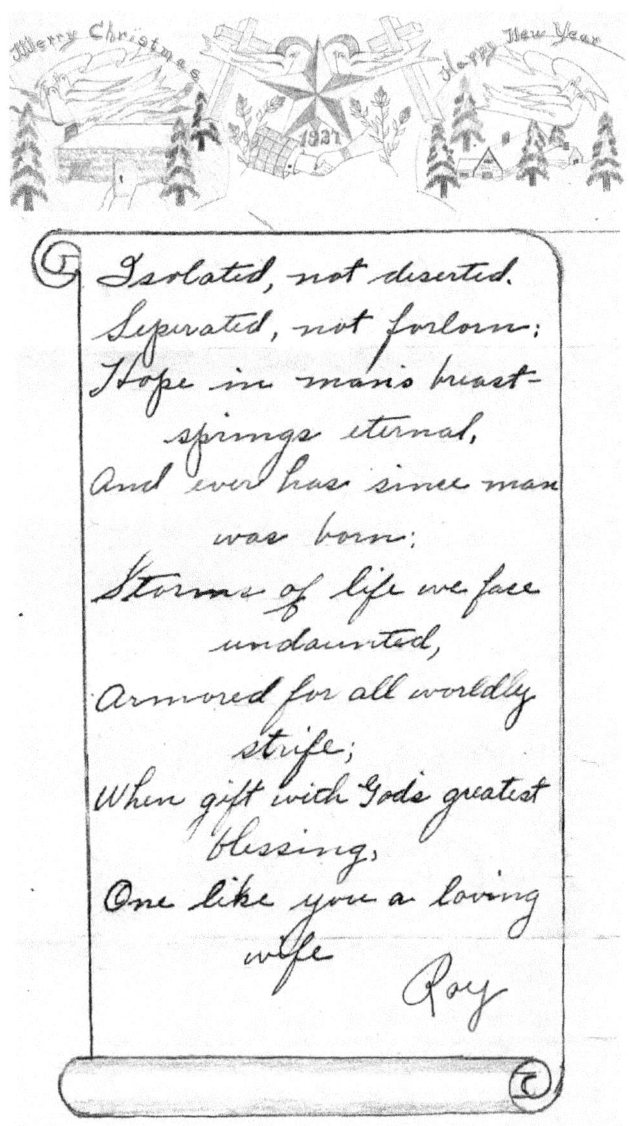

Isolated, not deserted.
Seperated, not forlorn;
Hope in man's breast—
    springs eternal,
And ever has since man
    was born;
Storms of life we face
    undaunted,
Armored for all worldly
    strife;
When gift with God's greatest
    blessing,
One like you a loving
    wife
                Roy

There is no record or memory preserved as to how that first Christmas passed with Roy behind bars. We don't know whether prisoners were allowed visitors on special holidays in addition to the alternate Sunday visits and whether Elise with or without Patricia were able to visit.[327]

Roy was confined but not alone. Throughout December, his convicted cohorts joined him at McNeil to serve their sentences as well. On December 30th, Roy's most loyal boat captain, Prosper Graignic, pleaded guilty to conspiracy in the Second Olmsted case and in the pending conspiracy case against George Comstock, the former Seattle policeman. He was sentenced to three years at McNeil Island Penitentiary.[328]

Interlude

Roy's last hope now to get out of prison was his pending petition to the Supreme Court for either a rehearing or reconsideration. Rarely granted, it was no surprise to anyone when the Supreme Court denied the rehearing request on January 3, 1928. But a week later on January 9th, the Court shocked everyone, especially the government, when the Justices issued a new order granting the writ of certiorari limited solely to the issue of the constitutionality of wiretapping.[329]

As soon as word reached Seattle of the Supreme Court decision to review Roy's conviction, his lawyer Paul Carrigan took steps to secure Roy's release.[330] Judge Neterer, to whom a petition for release was made, refused to recall the commitment until he received official notification from the Court and bonds were posted.[331] Roy was released from McNeil Island penitentiary on January 30th.

Roy posted $15,000 in bonds for his freedom pending the outcome of the Supreme Court review.[332] He was met at the dock in Tacoma by Elise, reporters and the U.S. Marshal to take him to King County jail where he had to post an additional bond for his further release while awaiting his trial in the Second Olmsted case, which he skipped out on earlier.[333]

It would take Elise a few more days to raise the additional $12,000 in bonds to secure Roy's release. Roy told the waiting reporters that he intended to force a quick trial on the charges in the Second Olmsted case so he could start with a clean slate. Roy made it clear that he was going straight.

He told reporters that he may have to go back to jail because of what he had done in the past, but it would not be "because of any future transgressions, because there won't be any." A familiar voice broke in and said, "Better kiss Patsy!" It was Elise there to meet him with their daughter Patricia.[334] It was a reminder of what was at stake in the future if he didn't go straight.

It is important to pause here to make a point about Roy's state of mind as this interlude began. Elise's iron-willed efforts to reform him and get him out on appeal, parole or pardon, were driving the legal strategy. It is often said that Roy came out of prison a different man due to his conversion to the Christian Science religion. That's true, but it overlooks the fact that Roy went into prison a different man too – he was done with bootlegging and that's down to Elise.

Elise's strategy to secure Roy's release included Roy using whatever leverage he had from his knowledge of who got paid what bribes. It was reported when Roy was released that he intended to "bare every secret of his past life."[335] The newspaper reported that the statement came from an authoritative source and that "all" meant that Roy would "have much to say concerning various officials, high and low, with whom he contacted in his operations."[336] The authoritative source almost certainly was Elise. In the same article, the reporter described Elise as working for Roy's freedom, and described her as "the militant, fighting Elise who raised the bond that opened the prison gates."[337]

The government was unmoved by the "tell all" threats and the insinuation that Roy "has something which will reflect upon the integrity of the law enforcement officers of the government."[338] Whitney sarcastically asked: "Has he meditated over the situation during the months he was at McNeil Island and is he now ready to clean up this whole rotten mess? I doubt it very much."[339]

But in fact Roy had meditated about being in jail and wanted to get his freedom as much as Elise wanted him out too. Elise finally was able to raise all of the bond money.[340] On February 5th, they headed home, which was no longer their mansion in Mount Baker but an "uptown hotel."[341] Along the way, he walked back his "tell all" threats and told reporters he resolved two things: to jump no more bail and "to refrain from airing his plans without advice from counsel."[342]

As to the second resolution, Roy said:

> *My plan is not one of reprisal. All I want is my liberty as soon as I can get it. I don't want to go out of my way to make enemies. My purpose in the future is to cultivate the good will of my codefendants. For any further statement of my plans, see my lawyer, John Dore.*[343]

We don't know for sure why Roy replaced his lawyer, Paul Carrigan, with John Dore, but Elise almost certainly was behind it. She was against letting Carrigan handle the Woodmont Beach case and Supreme Court writ. She wrote to someone in Washington, D.C., named Paul Bradshaw for advice about John Dore and she received a very supportive letter in reply and offer of hospitality for Dore when he came to Washington to argue the case.[344]

The switch was not easy because Carrigan, perhaps rightly, felt he had done a very creditable job. The day after Roy's release from jail, on February 6, he sued Roy for his fees, totalling $2400.[345] Roy asserted that he never agreed to pay Carrigan and had refused to sign a note for payment:

> *Paul came to me in the county jail and said he believed he could get me out of serving the McNeil Island sentence by appealing the case. I told him I would not spend a nickel, that I'd have to go to the house of fallen angels. I told him if he wanted to go ahead with the case personally that it was all right with me.*[346]

Carrigan had gone ahead with the work anyway. The case would go to trial in May.[347] Elise and Roy both testified in the case, but the jury found for Carrigan and Roy was ordered to pay $1000.

Elise was not happy with the outcome and made her feelings known:

> *I gathered witnesses in the smuggling case and outlined Roy's defense. I also took the initiative in the appeal to the Supreme Court. I did everything except actually represent Roy in court, and I would have done that had I been a lawyer.*[348]

But Elise got what she wanted. It was John Dore who headed to Washington, D.C., to argue the brief before the Supreme Court on February 20, 1928. It's no surprise that the case garnered national attention.

Not unlike today, the Justices interrupted and quizzed the lawyers for both sides. The newspapers reported that "[s]o sharp and persistent were these questions from the bench that neither [counsel were] able to follow any sustained line of argument very far."[349] After the arguments, observers said the Court leaned two ways and the Justices were split.[350] The decision would not come until the last day of the term four months later.

Maybe it was a sense that the Court was not fully leaning in favor of Roy that led one of Roy's bondsmen to believe that Roy was going to flee the city, listening to a false rumor.

At the end of February, the bonding company called Roy into their offices downtown and told him that its bond was withdrawn.

In a "spectacular attempt to escape," Roy fled down nine flights of stairs only to be caught at the door and brought to court where a bench warrant for his arrest was issued on withdrawal of the bond.[351] Elise was unable to obtain the necessary $7000 substitute bond, so Roy found himself yet again in the King County jail. He spent two nights there before Elise could arrange the necessary surety.[352]

No Escape

Roy could not escape the long tail of the bootlegging cases in the interlude while the Supreme Court considered his case. He certainly had his own problems as noted, but there still were bootlegging matters to resolve for the government. One of those matters involved the investigation of Al Hubbard.

On March 5, 1928, in a room at the Olympic Hotel in Seattle, Roy secretly met with government special agents who were investigating the claims against Hubbard who, as a Prohibition agent, was getting paid from both sides. Hubbard had been suspended from the Prohibition agency for nearly a year as the charges were investigated. Now near the end of the inquiry, and with Roy having reason to talk, the investigation was coming to a head.

Roy said that he never personally paid off the Big Four: Lyle, Whitney, Revelle and Corwin, but that he had given Hubbard money to do so. Roy gave the agent a signed affidavit alleging large payments to Hubbard in 1926 and 1927.[353]

A grand jury was convened, but Whitney and Revelle sought to protect Hubbard. After all, Hubbard was a key witness in pending cases and was too important of a witness for the government to lose in ongoing prosecutions, let alone considering the impact on past cases. With the help of Revelle and Whitney, Hubbard beat the charges.[354]

Revelle now pushed forward with three pending cases, announcing on March 24, 1928, that he was ready to go to trial.[355] The first case was against the former head of the Seattle police Dry Squad, George Comstock, and the bootleg distributors Frank and John Gatt, commenced on March 25, 1928. Known as the Little Comstock case, the Gatt brothers were alleged to have paid Comstock as much as $1000 per week for protection.[356] Roy was not involved directly in this case, but it was a reminder of graft and bribery that Roy so masterfully deployed.

The government made its case and rested on March 28th when, unexpectedly, the Gatt brothers changed their plea to guilty. The court immediately entered a sentence of one year at McNeil Island penitentiary and the remainder of the case, including Comstock, went to the jury.[357] After twelve hours of deliberation, the jury acquitted the remaining defendants.[358]

The so-called Big Comstock case was next up and again included in the trial Lieutenant George Comstock with eight other policemen accused of conspiring with Roy and others in the bootleg trade commenced on May 18, 1928. The government's chief witness was Herb Fletcher, several times indicted as the rum-running partner of Roy, but never tried. At the time of the case, he was a deputy sheriff in Port Townsend, Washington. The paper described him perfectly: "a confident young man who took a clean back dive into a five-year-old pool of booze and graft, splashed around a while - and emerged somewhat less confident."[359]

The government also called Richard Elbro, Roy's former bookkeeper, who came from Vancouver, B.C., to testify. Just as his wife, Ruth, who voluntarily testified against Elise in the Whispering Wires trial, Dick volunteered to testify about the amount of money that flowed through the enterprise.[360] The defense called the testimony what it was – payment for the future "right to live in the United States."[361]

Fletcher testified that he had seen Comstock, in uniform, at Roy's home on several occasions. But the defense called Elise, who flatly denied there were any such meetings at her home, nor had she ever received any phone calls from Comstock. On cross-examination, Revelle tried to get Elise to admit that Roy was in the bootleg business. She made for a tough witness. She would only admit that he was in the liquor business in Vancouver, B.C., and that "he was in the radio business" in Seattle.[362] In a stinging defeat for Revelle and the government, Comstock and all the officers were acquitted.

The Big Comstock case probably was the last time that Roy and Elise protected one of Roy's cohorts. Despite the government's loss, and the jury's seeming disinterest in convicting public officers, Revelle and the government would have some good news in just a few days.

On June 4, 1928, the Supreme Court, in a 5-4 decision, upheld Roy's conviction and the constitutionality of wiretapping. Revelle and the Prohibition agents were "elated" because Roy finally would have to return to prison to serve his term and all the conversations collected by wiretapping during the past investigations could be used in the pending cases. Any appeals of prior cases on those grounds would now fail.[363]

Roy at least would have a few days with Elise while awaiting the commitment papers to return to McNeil Island. On June 21st, Roy and Elise appeared in the Marshal's office and Elise pronounced "here's your prisoner. I brought him here as early as I could."[364]

A Golden Opportunity

A digression is necessary here. As already noted, Roy was committed to making his way in the world legitimately – he went into prison a changed man. In the interlude while the Supreme Court considered Roy's case between January and June 1928, a golden opportunity arose for Roy and Elise that they believed could give him that chance.

The Butte Boys Mining Company was incorporated February 6, 1928. On March 8, 1928, George W. Bever, its president, was in Seattle raising money to develop and operate the new Crown Peak mine in Bagby, California.[365] Mr. N. I. Logus, a Seattle broker, was identified as the responsible fundraiser for the financing.[366]

It is unclear whether Logus or Bever knew Roy or how Roy got involved with the project, but on April 20, 1928, he entered into an agreement with Harold Bever "for the purpose [of] acquiring by purchase, trade or location mines or mining claims in the United States, Canada and Alaska and the selling and the disposing of the same, and dealing in shares of stock in mining corporations and other securities of such corporations."[367] The agreement was witnessed and signed by "Elise Olmstead."

A Pre-Listing Offering of Shares in the Butte Boys Consolidated Mining Corporation was prepared with a capitalization of 2.5 million shares at ten cents per share. Bever was listed as president. The intent was to list the company on various stock exchanges. Elise had obtained her stockbrokers certification and she was listed as Fiscal Agent on the offering document as "E.C. Olmstead," perhaps to disguise her gender.

The offering is described as "A Real Project – Not a Promotion" and the shares offered "as an attractive speculation."

We know that Roy wanted to go to California to see the property. Bever wrote to him on April 26th from a hotel in San Francisco about it, but the property deal seemed to be in flux. Bever told him not to rush.[368] Roy couldn't rush. He was under bond in Seattle and not authorized to leave the state. Whether Bever knew anything at all about Roy's history and status is unknown.

Another letter, dated April 27, 1928, from another business partner, a Mr. Henry, located in Tacoma, Washington, was sent to Roy as well. Things were not going well, apparently due to statements made about Roy by one "Mr. L." who, it seems reasonable to conclude was Mr. Logus, the person responsible for raising funds for the mining venture:

> *Dear R.O. This will also be to your good wife, as she wrote me a note yesterday. She certainly wrote hastily because she did not understand my letter, for from the fourth to seventh lines, I did not intimate you were a liar, furthermore, I have repeatedly told everyone, including you and her that I did not believe you would lie - not even to save your neck, and I still believe. But given the statements made by Mr. L. and others, as they came to me, it was my duty as a friend, to tell you. The situation was fast taking a serious turn due to the fact that it appeared Mr. L. had spent the Mine funds and could not render an accounting and did not until serious steps were about to be taken, and in fairness to you, and to Mr. L., it was my duty to so advise of the situation, rather than remain silent....[369]*

The letter goes on to discuss a serious dispute among the parties involved in the mine, including Roy, and the refusal of one of the parties to agree to Roy being paid anything: "Also, if I rightly understand him, he will not consent your being paid $10,000 cash to waive 50,000 shares." Henry apparently wants out of the incorporation and asks Roy for his help and advice, but says, "Mrs. O refuses that you do so."

Henry says that Mr. L has dropped any relations with Roy. Henry says, "I think your wife is right and that in the end you will benefit by not dealing with him, if he has done what she says he did and does do." In closing, Henry says that he hopes Roy had heard favorably from Washington, a clear reference to the pending case before the Supreme Court.

There are no records or letters to explain these exchanges, but there are a few interesting points to be made. First, Roy needed money and he was trying to get $10,000 out of this operation in lieu of shares that he apparently had acquired or contractually was entitled to receive.[370] Second, Elise was very active in the ongoing business dealings, writing letters and staking out positions. And third, while this investment may have been a chance for Roy to go straight, especially if the Court overturned his conviction, one wonders whether those raising capital believed Roy was a conduit to launder the proceeds of bootlegging. Or conversely, whether the fundraisers were unaware of the cloud hanging over Roy and his lack of funds and therefore angry at whatever representations Roy or Elise made to them.

In any event, Roy plainly felt the need to make a trip to California. On May 4th, he asked Judge Neterer for permission to make a business trip to California for ten days. One bondsman refused to consent so Judge Neterer told Roy he would grant the request if Roy got the bondsman to agree.[371] Roy convinced the bondsman somehow and departed for California to the great entertainment of the newspapers that wrote "Roy Olmsted [was] to Become a Miner as He Awaits Trial."[372]

An engineering drawing and projection of the mining operations was prepared by S. A. Matthews on May 20, 1928, showing the vein to be exploited in the Crown Peak Mine, which is located in Mariposa County, California, as well as the average price per ton to be extracted.[373] Indeed it was a real project.[374]

When the Supreme Court disappointed Roy and Elise on June 4th, and it was clear that Roy would serve his sentence, he signed a brief termination letter on June 9th of all agreements involving the Butte Boys mine: "All agreements entered into heretofore between H.H. Bever, Roy Olmstead, and the Butte Boys Consolidated are this day canceled."[375]

Apparently, Roy continued to hold shares in the mine, yet it was not paying out anything. Elise alluded to as much in comments to a reporter in August 1930 when she was asked directly whether Roy was going to take care of his mine when his sentence was up:

> *"The mine is doing very well but they refused to turn Roy's stock over to me even if I did have his power of attorney. And I'm afraid we've got to go to court before we realize anything from it. No. Roy's not going down to the mine. He'll stay here a little while, I think."*[376]

One more aside here. How the media knew about Roy's involvement with Butte Boys mine is unknown. Why they thought it was "his mine" also is unknown and certainly an exaggeration of his position. Thirdly, inasmuch as Roy still owed a fine of $8000 to the government and the Internal Revenue Service was still looking for his bank accounts to cover over $100,000 in back taxes they claimed he owed, it is inexplicable that the government did not seize whatever shares Roy held.

In March 1931, Elise was called as a witness in a civil lawsuit brought by S.A. Matthews, the Seattle mining engineer listed on the offering, against the Butte Boys mining company for $750 for the survey and report prepared in June 1928 on the mining properties owned and operated by the company in California.

The company claimed that Roy and his wife were responsible for the employment of Matthews and the bill should be paid by them. Elise testified that neither she nor Roy had anything to do with hiring Matthews, and that their only connection with the Butte Boys company was "as brokers for the sale of stock which they purchased at 5 cents a share and disposed of for what they could get."[377]

The newspapers did not report the outcome of the trial, and it is not a reported case, but it seems likely that Roy or Elise hired Matthews to at least prepare the mining drawing to further the potential for sale of their shares. Roy was broke, so Matthews probably was quite happy to have Elise place the obligation squarely on the mining company.

Roy was returned to prison, but the gold mining dream continued throughout Roy's confinement. As we will see, after Roy's release from prison in 1931, he continued to pursue it, but it came to nothing. We have no record of the disposition of Roy and Elise's interest in the mining company.

PART V

Elise Alone

ELISE ON HER OWN

R oy was philosophical about his return to prison, talking to reporters along the way on June 21, 1928:

"Every bootlegger goes into the game for one thing – the dollar. That's what I did. But it cannot pay, and never will. A man might violate a law for quite a while, and make huge profits, but unless he pulls out of it he will be caught and punished."

"I have lost my home and my money. But when I come out, I am going to apply my energies and abilities to some lawful activity. And, [with an affectionate squeeze of his wife's arm] with the help of the best little pal in the world, I am going to be a success."[378]

And with that, Roy commenced serving his four-year sentence, and Elise was alone. John Dore still filed one more petition with the Court for rehearing, perhaps thinking the general public sentiment against the Court's decision might have given one or more of the Justices pause.[379] It failed, as expected.[380]

Roy now wanted to put all of his legal troubles behind him and concentrate on his future. The first thing he needed to do was resolve the still pending Second Olmstead case. Roy asked the court for an immediate trial and planned to plead guilty to the charge.[381]

On November 21, 1928, Roy was brought over from McNeil Island to appear before Judge Bourquin in federal court to enter his plea. He was sentenced to 13 months in prison to run consecutively with his current sentence from the Whispering Wires trial. All of those convicted in the Second Olmsted case had their sentences run concurrently, which was a bitter pill for Revelle and Whitney to swallow. What was the sense in bringing the case, they asked. But for Roy, as he said: "That finishes it."[382]

Elise was there to be with Roy when he arrived at court to enter his plea.[383] Roy's parents and his sister Sallie were also there, waiting for him in the Marshal's office. There was no mention in the newspapers of whether Patricia was there this time. It was a short visit and with that, Roy returned to prison.[384]

Roy left court with no charges hanging over his head and told reporters that he intended to seek parole when eligible, which would be after one-third of his sentence had been served. Not counting the initial two months he spent in prison before the Supreme Court took up his case, Roy stood at the five-month mark. He would head back that night to McNeil Island to face a long winter ahead, if not several winters. Elise had brought Roy's heavy winter coat and hat. She explained to reporters: "He left here in the summer wearing summer clothing. He needs his overcoat now."[385]

Now Elise had to find work while also caring for a young child. She had to make a hard decision, and given what we now know about her giving up her first child for adoption, this must have been particularly painful. She decided to send Patricia away to live with a Scottish couple, the McLeod's, while she went to work full-time. Almost 90 years later, that separation was still upsetting for Patricia, leaving her with a profound sense of abandonment.[386]

John M. MacLeod was 45 years old and Bertha B. McLeod was 38, without children of their own. Patricia remembered them being Canadian with John selling insurance for Sun Life, a Canadian Life Insurance company. She recalled that he would take her with him sometimes to meet his clients. They were very good to her, in her memory, and they lived modestly during this time in Seattle.[387]

It would be too easy to judge Elise at this point. She had to work full-time and earn enough to keep going. She was essentially the young wife of a convicted felon alone in the world with a small child where women were not paid to be the primary source of household income. She had no other means of support while Roy was in jail, and by 1930, the Great Depression had started. There was no hidden pot of money, contrary to popular belief. As she said about her life at this time, "one must live."[388] Needs must.

She was not yet thirty years old, but if she had learned anything in life, it was that she was resilient, resolute, and resourceful. She had to be now because she had no family near to help support her. She had not been in contact with her siblings since she left England over ten years earlier. In fact, as far as we know, they didn't know where she was or what happened to her, and that may well have been Elise's intent in leaving in the first place.

Roy's family had nothing to do with Elise from the time of the breakup of Roy's first marriage, or with Patricia for that matter.

Besides, Roy's parents were nearing the end of their lives.[389] However, they certainly had the means to provide some financial support, but apparently, they did not make the effort.

Roy's brothers Ralph and Frank both were still close to Roy and had solid jobs with the police. They would visit Roy in jail despite their embarrassment, but likewise they apparently did not provide any support for Elise and Patricia either. The same is true with Roy's sister, Sallie, who was single and ran the successful family real estate business, Olmsted Realty, after their father retired.[390] Why not bring Elise into that successful business? Even in the Depression, one gets the impression that Elise could have sold shacks in Hooverville to anyone if given the chance.

Maybe they all offered to help but Elise refused out of pride. Patricia didn't think so. Maybe they didn't because they blamed Elise for the breakup of Roy's first marriage or his wayward life. We just don't know. What we do know is that in the end, Elise and Patricia remained outcasts without support from Roy's family. And that separation would carry through Patricia's life as well to the point that her children didn't even know that they had cousins living in Seattle.[391]

And finally, we don't know how Roy felt about "the arrangement" with Patricia and the McLeod's either. He left no letters about it. But he and Elise must have discussed it during Elise's visits. Prisoners at McNeil Island Penitentiary were allowed to receive visitors twice a month on alternate Sundays in the basement of the Administration building, separated from each other by a wire screen wall. Elise is said to have been such a frequent visitor that the guards knew her by name and regularly escorted her back to the prison launch.[392] But when she left after each visit, Elise was still on her own.

Seeking Parole

Roy and Elise probably hoped that the arrangement with Patricia and the McLeod's while Elise searched for work would be short-lived. They probably believed that he would be granted parole when first eligible in August 1929. After all, others involved in the conspiracy had been granted an early release and Roy was cooperating with the government.

Elise always thought that Roy's knowledge of the corruption in the City could be the key to his early release, and his cooperation with the government would be essential to his parole. So Roy began meeting with the government in the McNeil Island penitentiary in the Fall of 1929. Word filtered out.

The newspapers shouted, "Roy Olmsted, convict rum racketeer, has 'told it all.'"[393] Roy's affidavit, the paper said, reveals whom he paid and how much, "in figures running close to $250,000 in one deal alone."[394] Who convinced Roy to tell all? The paper reported "[t]he principal figure behind Olmsted's new move is said to be Mrs. Elsie Olmsted, his wife, who has labored ceaselessly in his behalf since he went to McNeil Island penitentiary two years ago."[395]

But Roy and Elise would be disappointed. His parole was denied in January 1930 due to the seriousness of his offenses. Revelle's replacement as U.S. Attorney after his retirement, Anthony Savage Sr., did not support Roy's parole even though Roy understood that he would not oppose it.[396] At the time of Roy's guilty plea in the

Second Olmsted case, Roy met with Savage after sentencing. Savage reportedly told Roy he would not approve any application for a pardon, but Savage said, "I would not make an active fight against one."

It must have dawned on Roy and Elise now that there would be no early release for Roy and he would serve his entire sentence. His only hope to restore his rights now and start anew was a Presidential pardon. And that's exactly what the indefatigable Elise would throw herself into obtaining for Roy while at the same time she had to work to survive.

So what jobs did Elise do? She first worked as a nurse. There are two photos of her in a nurse's uniform from April 1929 taken in Seattle, but it is unclear whether she actually was trained as a nurse.[397] In any event, it was a short-lived profession as Roy's notoriety carried over to limit her opportunities. Elise described the situation with obvious bitterness: *"I had good positions here after Roy's imprisonment [she is a nurse] and would have kept them, but lady patients would find out who I was and object. And out I would go. Whitney and McKinney did that for me."*[398]

By 1930, she was working as a traveling saleswoman out of Salt Lake City. She told a reporter: *"I have no home now. I just stay at hotels and eat in restaurants."*[399] There is no record of the company she worked for or the nature of the products she sold. Patricia and her grandchildren also recall that she traveled and worked for Pinkerton at some point in those years, but again, there is no record of it.[400]

It is unclear exactly how long the arrangement with the McLeod's lasted, but Patricia was back home with Elise when Roy completed his sentence in 1931. It is equally unclear whether Elise saw Patricia at all during that time, on weekends or evenings, or whether her early jobs kept her away or out of town. Those details are lost to time and Patricia's childhood memories.

Whitney-Lyle Graft Trial

Just because Roy and his cohorts went to prison did not mean that the illicit liquor trade ended, especially as Hubbard remained free and there was plenty of money to pay bribes. But Hubbard was desperate to regain his good standing as a Prohibition agent and he let it be known that Lyle, Whitney, Agent Corwin and Revelle all were accepting graft and could be caught.[401] The Department of Justice and the Federal Bureau of Investigation, with Hubbard's assistance, began investigating all of them.

As part of the investigation, the FBI interviewed Roy, his co-conspirators, minor bootleggers with whom Whitney had clashed, and many of the agents who worked with Whitney. A grand jury convened on May 17, 1930, to consider the vast volume of evidence collected from just about everyone that had an ax to grind against the four of them. Hubbard, now the confessed liquor ring organizer, was the first to testify and told the grand jury that "he paid $150,000 to 'grease official palms' of city, state and county officials."[402]

Word got out that Roy would be a witness on the morning of May 20th, and Elise also would be called as a witness. The newspaper, no doubt glad to have Roy back in the headlines to sell papers, declared "Home Town Boy, Who Became Booze King Comes Back, Smiling, With Bodyguard."[403] The article is accompanied by a photo of Roy posing before the door marked "Grand Jury." As the paper put it, he was brought over from McNeil Island to "'tell all,' for the first time, in the government's efforts to pin indictments on any of its officers who may or have been 'corrupt,'"[404]

Remarkably, Roy was able to walk around the town while waiting to testify:

> *[T]here was his wife, Elise, beside him as he made his way about town, with a prison guard in civilian clothes keeping a discreet distance…. Old friends stopped him and shook his hand, he walked along familiar streets and along the familiar corridors of the Federal Building, where six years ago a federal jury broke his power.*[405]

Roy testified for over two hours and allegedly "told all." What he said exactly was not revealed. Exciting as this prospect was of finding out who was behind the entire liquor ring – the "mysterious leader" who allegedly animated Roy,[406] it was Elise that drew the most attention:

> *Mrs. Olmsted waited about the building. She had been with Roy since his arrival and she was perhaps the main reason why Roy thought the old home town looked pretty good.*
>
> *She wore a white fur coat. Some thought it was the same fur coat she wore in the palmy days. Others said it looked like new.*[407]

But then she was called to testify. And it caused a stir:

> *Mrs. Olmsted's sudden entrance into the jury room caused a ripple of surprise among spectators and federal officials crowding the corridor. She had said she would not testify—that there would be no use calling*

her, but womanlike apparently, she changed her mind and when her husband left the stand. . . she walked through the well-guarded door.

She did not stay long – only about fifteen minutes – and what she told, no one knows.

"It wasn't important," she told newspaper men. "Really, it was of little consequence."[408]

Before testifying, Elise freely admitted that a large sum of money had been paid to a member of Revelle's staff to keep her out of the picture. "Roy," she told reporters, "paid plenty — they bled him dry and then threw him down."[409] In the grand jury room, Elise reportedly told the jury that "certain officials agreed not to prosecute her in the Olmsted conspiracy case – for a consideration."[410] The person on Revelle's staff ultimately was revealed to be Assistant U. S. Attorney McKinney.

On May 23, 1930, after six days of secret testimony, the grand jury indicted Whitney, Lyle, Corwin, Fryant and McKinney on twenty counts of bribery and conspiracy to violate the National Prohibition Act.[411] Whitney and Lyle were suspended without pay on May 27th; Corwin was penniless and had just been released from the hospital in Hawaii to return to Seattle. McKinney was nowhere to be found.

McKinney surrendered to Department of Justice agents in San Francisco on June 4, 1930, claiming he was staying with friends and was unaware of the indictment. He said he learned of it through the press, made arrangements for his bond and then surrendered. He denied the charge that Olmsted had given him $6000 to keep Elise out of the whispering wires trial.[412]

But the next day, McKinney let it be known that he would not return to Seattle and would fight extradition. Apparently, McKinney was tipped off to the indictment a few hours before its announcement and jumped the first train south. He had believed that he knew too much to ever be indicted, which begs the question about how much there was to know about government graft.[413]

McKinney's legal machinations were imaginative if anything. He moved to have Roy brought to San Francisco to testify in his extradition proceeding, which was set for June 18th, at his own expense.[414] McKinney failed to post the funds to bring Roy to San Francisco, so Seattle U.S. Attorney Savage stepped in to bring Roy as a government witness. When Roy arrived at the hearing, McKinney was surprised.[415] His gambit had backfired.

Roy's testimony was sensational. He said he paid McKinney $3000 to further the ambitions of Revelle to run for governor and in return, McKinney told Roy that his phones were being wiretapped. Roy said that McKinney told him the donation would be "government insurance" and $3000 would be just about the right amount. He also said that he delivered bottles of gin to McKinney and payments of $50 or $100, but stopped paying him when he decided he was no longer needed. Roy said, besides, "[h]e was ginning us to death."[416]

McKinney dropped his opposition to extradition the next day.[417] He returned to Seattle a week later to enter his not guilty plea and stand trial.[418] The trial date was set for August 12, 1930.

The trial was every bit as engaging as Roy's Whispering Wires trial four years earlier. Hubbard was the key witness. The trial was a tragedy for the five loyal government servants. Hubbard's testimony boiled down essentially to the claim that Roy urged him to get into the Prohibition office and to bribe Lyle, Whitney and others, and then, having corrupted these men, paid them the money Roy provided for protection.[419]

It must have become patently obvious that Hubbard was keeping the money and making both sides think they were getting what they wanted. Whitney was getting Hubbard's regular reports on the flow of liquor and Roy thought he was getting protection for the imports. Hubbard managed both sides' expectations perfectly and profited all the more. Indeed, the defense sought to prove that Hubbard, "self-styled go-between, who collected protection payments from bootleggers for Federal officials had kept all the money for himself."[420]

Roy spent two days on the stand. He had a rough go of it. You can read the summary of his testimony and follow the cross-examination in the newspapers, but there probably is only one true statement in the entire testimony – that Roy previously stated that he was never able to corrupt Whitney and Lyle.[421] The statements were made to two different government representatives and offered as impeachment at trial. To Prosecuting Attorney Colvin, Roy said in November 1926: "I've paid plenty of protection to county and city officers, but I was never able to reach Whitney. He's a fanatic and he used unfair methods against me by tapping my telephone." And to U.S. Marshal Laird in November 1927, he said: "Whitney and Lyle are two honest prohibition men. I never was able to reach them."[422]

The trial lasted thirty-six days. All sides were exhausted, and likely the newspaper reporters and readers were exhausted too. Would it never end? Fifteen years of Prohibition in Washington State and the booze still flowed like water. Just before midnight on September 20th, the jury found all four of the defendants not guilty.[423] No doubt, the repeated admissions of Hubbard to lying in many of the prior cases were enough to eradicate any doubt, let alone a reasonable one, that he was telling the truth now.

McKinney was the fifth defendant and he did not have to wait until the end for his verdict of not guilty. Elise had testified that she had accompanied Roy on car rides downtown to pay McKinney, but she had never actually seen McKinney or the payment. Mary Alexander, Elise's nurse during 1924-25, similarly testified to going for such drives but likewise had not seen the payoff.[424] Only Roy's testimony stood as to the alleged graft.

On McKinney's motion for a directed verdict, the court took to be true that Roy had bribed him, but concluded that the statute of limitation had long run on those acts and that McKinney was not otherwise implicated in the broader conspiracy charged against Whitney and the others.[425]

That was it. The trials were over. Roy went back to prison to serve his remaining sentence, and Elise went back to her job to make ends meet.

PART VI

Elise and Roy, Together Again

ROY COMES HOME

On May 12, 1931, Roy was released from prison after serving 34 months of his four-year sentence. He arrived from McNeil Island to be greeted by Elise in their car to be driven back to Seattle. A few reporters were gathered at the landing to snap a picture of Roy smiling and Elise in the driver's seat, which the Seattle Post-Intelligencer printed along with a brief few paragraphs … on page 2. Roy was no longer front-page news, and he seemed happy with that as he told reporters that he was "definitely and finally through with bootlegging."[426]

Roy was 47 when he was released. He told reporters frankly that he didn't know what he would do other than try to make his way in Seattle.[427] They had no money at all and the Internal Revenue Service claimed $100,000 in back taxes. Elise was working. Patricia recalls being back home in their apartment when Roy returned. She would have been just shy of six years old.

In the midst of the Depression, and even with his old contacts and friends, work was hard to find. Two weeks after his release, on May 26, 1931, Roy boarded the steamship H. F. Alexander bound for San Francisco, ostensibly to look for work. He had not faded off the front page enough to avoid reporters calling at his house, looking for a story and trying to determine whether Roy was getting back into the game despite his denials. Roy's trip south was reported along with a quote from Elise that he was "going to California to look over business conditions there."[428]

Elise saved a letter Roy wrote to her from the ship. It is transcibed in Appendix II. It is clear from the letter that Roy was traveling with a purpose to Merced, California, and that purpose, no doubt, was to revive his interest in the Butte Boys mine. He had high but seemingly unfounded hopes. His Golden Opportunity, as discussed above, seems to have left him with whatever shares he and perhaps his brothers had purchased in the initial offering to try to sell in the midst of a Depression.

Some evidence of that outcome is in Roy's pardon application, which is discussed more broadly below. The investigating officer wrote of Roy's work history that his brothers Ralph and Frank were principal owners in the Butte Boys mine in Bagby, California, and that they employed Roy to sell stock in the mining claim, from June to October 1931.[429] Unfortunately, we have no record of the disposition of mining shares.

Roy took whatever work he could find, cleaning rugs for rent, part-time sales work for commissions, de-mothing and extermination services. His pardon application in 1935 lists a series of employers, each of whom endorsed Roy as reliable, honest and hard-working. He seldom earned more than $100 per month. But his fortunes changed when he joined the Retail Credit Service Bureau in the summer of 1935. The owner, a Christian Science adherent who encouraged Roy along his journey to faith, vouched for Roy's character and good behavior. He paid Roy $200 per month.

Roy barely made ends meet during those first few years. He persisted while Elise gathered all of the necessary support for a pardon application on his behalf.[430] The pardon application file at the National Archives exceeds 100 pages and contains dozens of supportive affidavits and statements in support of clemency, most of which were gathered by Elise.[431] Roy's clemency application was first made in mid-1934 but was returned as premature. His lawyer apparently was unaware of the Department of Justice's rules for pardon and the requirement that the applicant wait four years after parole to apply.

The delay in filing only made Roy's application better. Elise was tireless in organizing the application. Judge Neterer, former U. S. Attorney Revelle and former U. S. Attorney Savage, all of Roy's employers and landlords, and a host of others, attested to his reformed character. Revelle in particular felt enormous remorse after his retirement at having relied on the dishonest testimony of Hubbard in the bootlegging trials, and he believed that Roy should be restored to his civil rights. Whitney, of course, objected to Roy's clemency, but his bitterness over his own trial and bribery allegations discounted his opinion.

The investigating officer noted that Roy had refrained from alcohol and smoking, had no money and owned no real estate upon his discharge from prison, and had insufficient funds to pay his pending fine. The report provided a detailed summary of Roy's employment and where he and his family had lived during the time since his discharge. Roy and Elise moved frequently during those four years.[432] Their residence at the time of the application was the Wilsonian, which caused the investigator to note that "[t]hese apartment houses are high class," but Roy informed the reviewer that he worked at demothing and cleaning to offset his rent.

On Christmas Eve, 1935, the President of the United States, Franklin D. Roosevelt, granted Roy a presidential pardon with full restitution of his civil rights and remission of the claimed back taxes and fines. The Christmas Day headline on page 1 read: Wife Wins Pardon for Olmstead."[433] Roy gave all the credit for his pardon to Elise, saying "She's been wonderful. She's put me back on my feet." The reporter observed that Elise "modestly admitted" that she had devoted herself to winning Roy's pardon:

> *"It was lots of work," she confessed, "but it was worth it. I can't describe how happy it makes me to know that the slate has been wiped clean and that we can look everybody in the face again. "Why," she added, "he can vote now just like anybody else."[434]*

Lastly, Roy's journey to a pardon was made easier by his journey to the Christian Science faith. According to Roy's statements in support of his pardon application, it was a cellmate of his that raised his consciousness about his salvation and the church. Roy read avidly in prison, attended church and did not drink or smoke, according to the application. Then, when National Prohibition was repealed on December 5, 1933, Roy received a number of lucrative offers as a nightclub manager and liquor distributor. He turned them down.[435]

By all accounts, his faith was sincere. He frequently visited McNeil Island after his release, worked with alcoholics and prisoners throughout his life. Upon his death, his obituary mourned his loss as a Christian Science practitioner, noting that he maintained a Christian Science office in the Times Square building and worked with county jail prisoners for years.[436]

We don't know what Elise thought about Roy's conversion or his new subdued lifestyle. According to Patricia, her mother did in fact smoke and drink and maybe curse just a little, but she did not convert to Christian Science. She also did not take a vow of poverty. While times were tough everywhere, as the pardon application noted, they lived in a posh apartment in 1935. And from Roy's letter to her on his way to Merced to check on the mining opportunity after his release, it looked as if Roy had some convincing to do to leave her behind to save the cost of the trip. She still dressed well, and her life during these years was no less full. Fracture lines may well have started by this time.

A Domestic Life

Pursuing Roy's pardon consumed much of Elise's life in the first half of the decade of the 1930s, but Elise also threw herself into Patricia's school, and particularly, the Summit School Parent-Teacher Association. After a year of volunteer work at school events, she was elected President of the Summit School Parent-Teacher Association in November 1932, a position she would hold for six consecutive terms.

In April 1934, the newspaper printed a lovely photo of Elise, announcing that the Parent-Teacher Association was hosting a bridge luncheon in honor of Elise, its "popular and efficient president."[437]

A newspaper search for "E.C. Olmstead," the name she apparently used for her school activities, between 1932-1939, reveals dozens of newspaper announcements about various school activities in which Elise plays a very active role. Plus, she headed a Girl Scout Troop.

What is most interesting, apart from her apparently unbounded energy, none of the recognition or coverage described her as the bootlegger's wife. If an article called her "Mrs. Roy Olmsted," there was no further reference to Roy, his conviction, or rum running history. For the prior decade, she had no persona independent of Roy, but now, she was E.C. Olmstead, president of the PTA. One wonders if anyone in the PTA even knew of her or Roy's history.

The issue that most concerned Elise was the lack of a playground for the Summit School children. There was only a small concrete patch and Elise felt that the children needed a playfield. It was the only school in the district without one. It became her cause as President of the PTA in 1932 and continued for years, including in the courts.

In May 1934, she convinced the Seattle Conference of Parent-Teacher Associations to support a resolution that every school PTA press the Seattle City Council to approve funds for a playground for Summit School. Elise argued that most of the children had working mothers, with no adequate place to play during the school year or the vacation period. This, she said, resulted in a noticeable uptick in juvenile delinquency.[438]

The Summit School PTA's request was first presented to the School Board, then referred to the City's Park Board, which approved a resolution to purchase nine lots for the playground.[439] The resolution then was sent to the City Council. Elise organized a petition campaign with organizations like the American Legion backing the acquisition of the lots for the playground. Condemnation proceedings were begun and a jury set the acquisition cost at $113,500. The City Council then had six months to accept or reject the awards (which were based on City estimates without landowners contesting value).[440]

Six months turned into several more years as various parties sought to kill the project because it would have levied taxes on the neighboring owners to fund the acquisition. Some argued the school was archaic and would have to be replaced entirely so the park was not appropriate; others proposed downscaling the size; still others had odd proposals like a rooftop park on a nearby building. The matter ended up in Superior Court where Elise testified about the need for a park for child safety.

On November 12, 1938, the court found the proposed assessment in the condemnation proceeding to be arbitrary and without justification.[441] The assessment was ordered canceled and that ended the controversy, without a park. Over 500 property owners in the Summit district opposed the assessment.

Admittedly, the Summit School playground controversy does not compare to the Whispering Wires trial or other bootlegging trials for its excitement, issues of national importance, or drama, but in terms of understanding Elise, the years she spent fighting for the park speak volumes about her character. She did not give up. She was relentless. She was an effective and persistent advocate and skilled at getting others to advocate for her cause too. She never backed down. We don't know how Roy felt about her involvement in PTA or litigation, but one suspects he smiled and enjoyed his Elsie going at it hammer and tongs. But he also showed no personal interest in the fight.

Elise was also tireless in living her life to the fullest. She continued with her music and the arts. She was on the Executive Board of the Seattle Civic Opera Association and its Secretary and Manager in 1933. They presented four operas that season: Romeo and Juliet, Verdi's Masked Ball, and by her favorite composer, Wagner's Tannhauser and Lohengren.

It is unclear whether Elise was working in the first years of Roy's release, but she went to work full-time in 1936 for the City of Seattle courts. She first worked in the Traffic Violations Section for two years, and then worked directly for four years for the Judge of the Police Court. She left that job in 1942 in the midst of World War II to work for the War effort.

Ever the informer, at some point in 1936, Elise contacted the Federal Bureau of Investigation in Portland, Oregon, to report someone who was fraudulently obtaining Red Cross subscriptions and pocketing the money. The Special Agent in Charge of the office wrote to Elise in August 1936 to thank her and let her know that the man had been prosecuted, convicted and sentenced to six months in a federal road camp.[442]

Elise became a naturalized citizen on April 1, 1937. In her petition for naturalization, she stated that she lawfully entered the U.S. on November 16, 1920, under the name "Elsie Campbell." It is interesting to speculate about what prompted her desire to naturalize. Perhaps it was her experience in England during World War I, recognizing the importance of citizenship and its attendant rights in the face of a changing world and the rise of Nazi Germany. But she did not mark the occasion and her daughter Patricia noted that later, Elise destroyed her citizenship papers.

While working for the Police Court, in April of 1938, Elise applied for membership in the Seattle Police Revolver Club. She certified that she was a U.S. citizen and had never been convicted of a crime, both statements being literally true at the time. She became a new member in 1939 and paid her $5 membership fee. The application left blank any registration number for a weapon so it is unclear whether Elise actually owned a pistol.[443]

At some point, Elise was admitted to radio membership in the Corn Cob Pipe Club of Virginia. Radio Station WRVA in Richmond, Virginia, was one of many stations that had joined a network of broadcasters in the 1930s in the midst of the Depression to broadcast entertainment. They began broadcasting a traditional music show called the Corn Cob Pipe Club. The show was a mixture of comedy, popular and traditional songs, and even a minstrel duo

(Sawdust and Moonshine) based in a fictional town called Virginia Crossroads.

The show became immensely popular and "Corn Cob Pipe Club" chapters were formed in all 48 states at the time and by 1934 boasted over 272,000 members. The Corn Cob Pipe Club even published a monthly magazine called "Smoke" that went out to its members.[444] It's not surprising that Elise loved this idea given her abiding interest in radio and music, and yes, there was a Seattle chapter whose meetings were broadcast over KOMO radio, ironically, the successor station to Elise's KFQX a decade before.

At some point in 1939, Elise's sister Lily and brother Carl found her. We don't know how, but the result does not appear to be a rekindling of the family bonds. However, it was arranged that Patricia would visit Lily in Philadelphia that summer. Patricia traveled by train to Philly via Chicago where she stopped over to see her Aunt Florence along the way. Patricia was just fourteen and, remarkably, made the trip unaccompanied. Patricia clearly remembers the trip, visiting sites in Chicago from the World's Fair,[445] and arriving at her Aunt Lily's home, the address of which she correctly remembered some 85 years later when interviewed for this book. Lily's granddaughter recalls a few holiday cards being received for a few years after the visit, but then the family lost touch again.

As the decade closed, it is exhausting to read about all of the activities in which Elise was involved during the 1930s while working a full time job besides. It could not have left much time for Roy, or Patsy for that matter. It is almost as if Elise were making up for lost time when her life went from the Days of Opulence to being subsumed in Roy's prosecution and legal entanglements. Unlike the prior decade, they no longer appear as a couple at social events, gone are the extravagant dinners with notable people. Of course, it was the Depression too, but one cannot leave the decade without feeling that Roy and Elise were leading separate lives, and we know intuitively how that was going to end.

PART VII

Unraveled

Elise Alone Again

The breakup was not played out in public. There were no salacious stories, society page rumors or public displays of temper. It is clear that Elise needed an active social life, filled with music, art, and culture. It is also clear that Roy's spiritual awakening was filled with exactly the opposite things – people down on their luck, addicted to alcohol, looking for salvation instead of tickets to the next opera. He worked for a devout Christian Science man at the Retail Credit Service Bureau and spent his time outside of work with the church. It probably was not the life that Elise expected after working tirelessly to restore Roy's freedom and respectability.

So it was no surprise that Roy and Elise separated in 1940 over personal and religious differences.[446] Elise ultimately filed for divorce on May 29, 1943, on the grounds of desertion. Elise was living at 2435 41st St., and said in the divorce complaint that Roy had refused to live with her, without cause, since May 1, 1940.[447] The divorce was granted on August 5, 1943, without alimony, but Roy was ordered to pay $35 a month for Patricia until she came of age.[448]

It is not as if Elise was all alone when they separated as Patricia lived with Elise through the separation and divorce. Patricia was Class of 1943 at Broadway High School and turned 18 the week before the divorce was final. While her yearbook photo shows a smiling teenage girl, none of it was easy for Patricia. She was not a mere bystander to the events in her parents' lives yet she often felt that way. Add to that, Patricia says that she had little if anything to do with the Olmsted family after the divorce. She "felt like an outcast."[449]

At the time of their separation in 1940, Elise had been working full-time for the City of Seattle for over four years and supporting herself. The war in Europe had started in September 1939 with Germany's invasion of Poland and proceeded in earnest in May 1940 with Germany's swift advance through the Netherlands, Luxembourg, Belgium and into France. The start of the War in Europe had to hit her hard. She was still British at heart. And remember, she lost her older brother in the First World War and knew the tragedy of war firsthand.

But this World War was an order of magnitude worse. The Nazi air blitz of England began on September 7, 1940, when 348 German bombers and 617 fighters bombed London for two hours. The Seattle newspapers carried the story of the Blitz on the front page on September 8, 1940: *1,000 Attacking Planes Hurled Against Capital, London Areas Aflame in Biggest Raid.*"[450] The Battle of Britain would be front page news every day until May 1941 when Hitler shifted his focus to the war against Russia. In those 8 months of the Blitz, over 43,000 civilians were killed.[451]

Elise's family was in the midst of it. Her younger brother Carl still lived in London, as did her half-siblings and their families. Her sister Minnie lived in Liverpool. Though she had lost touch with her family since leaving London, one would think that she must have worried for them.[452] But strangely, there is no evidence among her keepsakes that she wrote or called her family or received word from them.

In September 1941, she qualified by written examination to enter the advanced course in motor mechanics under the auspices of the National Defense Ambulance Corps. It does not appear she ever pursued a specific job or posting, yet she kept the certificate among the few things she saved.

What was she thinking? Perhaps Elise had some vague idea about using her nursing skills in the Ambulance Corps in the war zone in Europe. She was living apart from Roy in 1940 although she was not yet divorced, and Patricia was still a teenager, but Elise was an independent woman and there is little doubt that if she decided to do it, she would have done so. But again, there is no record of her intention in taking the course or even her views about the War in Europe.

Then Pearl Harbor brought the U.S. into the War. The city of Seattle and indeed the entire Nation was transformed and put on a war footing overnight.

> *As the U.S. joined the war, mobs smashed downtown Seattle windows, local businesses sold bomb shelters, soldiers swarmed to guard Boeing, and Japanese Americans suddenly became outcasts in their own country.* [453]

For Elise, it must have felt like she was reliving the anti-German nightmare in Liverpool after the sinking of the Lusitania in World War I.

Did Elise feel the need to do something for the War effort? Because in the Fall of 1942, she decided to leave what was a secure and steady position with the municipal court that she held for over eight years and to apply for a job with the War Department and. She went to work as a clerk in the Overseas Supply Division, Operations Branch, in the Seattle Port of Embarkation, a job she held at least until the end of the War.[454]

The question now is whether Elise did anything more for the War effort. Recall from earlier discussion, that some believed, albeit wrongly, that Elise worked as a spy in World War I. And there was some hint, unproven, that perhaps she worked with the Office of Strategic Services or "OSS" in Seattle in some capacity in World War II. As noted previously, there is no record of any such employment in World War II, but her work as a civil servant at the Embarkation Port would not have precluded it either.

We just don't know for certain, but if anything, it seems more likely that she was a "volunteer" of information about those against the War just as she was in World War I or as an informant during Prohibition. Elise had shown over the years that she knew how to network and she was a joiner. For example, in February 1943, she joined the Washington State Press Club and was issued her press card, but again, to what purpose we do not know, but what better organization or network to gather information.[455]

The War marched into 1945. It would be months before there was victory in Europe in May 1945, and then the surrender of Japan in September. Seattle still enforced its blackout rules, but life and romance continued after the lights went out.[456]

Elise was no stranger, of course, to wartime romance. She knew the consequences firsthand in her own life. But she probably never expected it of her young daughter Patricia.[457] Elise was livid when Patricia married Roger Olin, a Lieutenant in the Navy, on March 1, 1945, a few months shy of her 20th birthday. Maybe she saw too much of her former self in Patricia's marriage to a military man at the end of the War. She intervened, and the marriage was annulled.

The subject is still tender when talking to Patricia. She said that she still resented Elise's obstinant interference. Patricia never wanted to be like her mother. Unlike Elise, Patricia neither drank nor smoked, which perhaps accounts in some measure for her sound mind and good health at ninety-nine years of age as of this publication. She is a true delight to talk to and readers can catch some of her sparkle in Ken Burn's *Prohibition* documentary.[458]

Roy's Life

If Elise established some degree of normalcy in the 1940s, those years were not kind to Roy. The separation and divorce from Elise was one thing, but on June 27, 1941, Roy's brother, Frank, a thirty-three-year veteran and a sergeant in the Seattle Police Department, took his own life. The newspaper reported that he shot himself in his car, which was parked a block from police headquarters. He had just reported back from a week of sick leave.

The death was ruled a suicide, and it was noted that he was depressed over financial matters, but the nature of those financial concerns was not disclosed.[459] Patricia remembered Frank as a "money maker." He allegedly made loans to city employees and others at a high interest rate, and he took up warrants from the City to its employees at steep discounts.

Patricia recalled Roy and Elise discussing him at the time of his death and saying that the "feds were closing in on him." She also recalled hearing that Frank put his money into diamonds to avoid the IRS.[460] Whatever the basis for these memories, there were no charges against him for wrongdoing.

It has always been an open question as to how involved Frank was with Roy in the bootleg business. It may be too much to say he was corrupt, but it is probably the case that he walked a fine line for his brother Roy and in his financial dealings. Whether any of those things were true or not, or contributed to his suicide, doesn't matter in the end; it was still a tragedy.

Patricia' s memories also suggest that, even though separated, Roy and Elise appear to have been on speaking terms after the divorce. Patricia did not recall attending any memorial service for Frank with Elise, however, or any other family events for that matter..

Frank was survived by his wife Sara and two sons. But tragedy struck again. Having lost her husband, Sara was to lose her eldest son, Frank Jr., in the War. In May 1944, Marine 2d Lieutenant Frank Olmsted Jr., a Marine fighter pilot, was killed in action in the Solomon Islands.[461]

Then, in 1946, Roy would lose his sister Sallie as well. Although ruled a suicide, her gruesome death was more than a little mysterious. Sometime in the early morning hours of December 19, 1946, about 40 miles east of Yuma, Arizona, Sallie covered herself in oil and burned herself to death in the car she was driving.[462]

Sallie was 62 years old, moderately wealthy, and a well-known and successful realtor in Seattle. Her brother Ralph told the newspapers that she had left Seattle in September in good spirits and he knew of no reason for her to commit suicide. But there was more to it than that.

It turned out that her sister Florence, who lived in Chicago, had filed an "insanity complaint" against her on September 3, 1946.[463] The complaint was dismissed the same day when all parties agreed that Sallie would be examined by two psychiatrists. The dismissal motion noted that Sallie had been a patient at Harborview hospital for seven days and hospital records showed no evidence of insanity.[464] Sallie left three days after the dismissal. She placed an ad in the newspaper stating that she was on vacation and that no one had any authority to incur obligations on behalf of Olmsted Realty except her.

The coroner's inquest ruled that Sallie set herself on fire in the car. A roll of cash was burned in the car including a $1000 bill, and there was no indication of anyone else around or in the car. Roy's brother Ralph brought the body back to Seattle, and that was the end of the inquiry.[465] But the inquest took two days of deliberation and apparently the jury heard evidence that Sallie had expressed fear for her life just days before the incident.[466] Until the Olmsted's put a stop to the inquiry by bringing Sallie's body back to Seattle, the Yuma County sheriff was looking for a man who apparently had accompanied Sallie from Seattle.

Sallie's demise is another Olmsted family story hidden away from public disclosure. Fair enough, there was enough publicity in Roy's life for the entire family. For her part, Patricia had only passing memories of these events, akin to having read about them in the newspaper. It is clear that neither she nor Elise had any meaningful relationship with Roy's family. While tragedies, the deaths and other events in Roy's family seem to have had little impact on their lives.

Roy died on April 30, 1966, of a heart attack at home in his Park Manor apartment on 13th Street in Seattle. He was 81. His remains were cremated and there were no memorial services at his request. His obituary was merely captioned "Science Practitioner," and while the short article acknowledged his bootlegging days and conviction, it stressed his conversion to Christian Science while in prison and the life of redemption he led after his pardon working with county jail inmates.[467] It is how he wanted to be remembered.

Elise's Last Years

Elise married Earl J. Swisher, a retired Lieutenant Commander in the Navy, on October 13, 1951, in Lewiston, Idaho. His nickname was "Swish." Earl was 65, Elise 51 – the age difference seemingly less relevant at that time of life than when Elise first met and married Roy. No one is certain how they met, but they were together for some time before they married.

Earl came from a large family from Kansas of five sisters and five brothers, none of whom apparently were at the wedding, which was a small service. Her daughter Patricia was one of the witnesses at the wedding, which took place before a Justice of the Peace in Lewiston, Idaho.

Both Elise and Swish indicated on the marriage license that they were previously divorced. But incredibly, on the marriage license,

Elise stated her maiden name as "Elsie Campbell." Recall that when she married Roy, she actually used "Parchè," not "Campbell." So even after all these years, Elise maintained the subterfuge about her real name.

Earl died October 25, 1959, in Bremerton, Washington. His brief obituary states he resided at 1631 39th Ave. N., in Bremerton and was survived by his "beloved wife" Elise and by "a daughter, Mrs. Donald McFarlane, Spokane," which is to say Patricia. There is no mention of his former wife or biological children. Elise arranged the funeral and prepared the obituary. While reading too much into any obituary is a risky business, in a way, Swish's obituary reflected Elise's "here and now" perspective on life. In Elise's world, Swish's life was with her, not his prior family, and Patricia and her two children at that time were named as Swish's daughter and grandchildren in the obituary, not his prior family members.

Elise was alone again after Swish died in 1959. She was fine financially, had access to the military exchange, and received Swish's pension and social security benefits. At this stage of her life, one would think that she would make an effort to visit or contact her sister Lily in Philadelphia, or Minnie or John in England, or any of her other relatives. It is especially odd after the effort Lily and John made to find and contact her in the late 1930s.

Indeed, Patricia even went to visit Lily in Philadelphia in 1939, alone at fourteen years old on a train across the country. Elise made no effort then to visit Philadelphia herself. Nor did go later in 1948 when her sister Minnie from England visited Lily for several months in Philadelphia. Whatever the rift or cause of separation between her and her siblings decades earlier, it must have been serious enough that Elise would never see them again. Lily died in 1961, Minnie in 1964, and John in 1971.

Still, Elise had her daughter and grandchildren, now numbering three, in Seattle. Perhaps that was enough for her. Elise's grandchildren have fond memories of her in the 1960s, often meeting her on the city bus coming or going someplace after school. They called her "Ikey" because, the story goes, when they were little, they couldn't pronounce the name Elise.

She lived the remainder of her life in relative obscurity, unlike Roy who became a legend during the 1960s, thanks in large part to Professor Norman Clark's article *Roy Olmstead, a Rumrunning King on Puget Sound* in The Pacific Northwest Quarterly in 1963. One wonders whether Elise read the article, and if so, what she thought about it. Apparently, Professor Clark interviewed Elise later when he turned the article into a book called *The Dry Years,* but he did not quote her at all in the book.[468] Other than that interview, there is no indication that Elise ever spoke about her days married to Roy or her other experiences to anyone.

Maybe she never found the words to tell the story of her past to her daughter or grandchildren. As Patricia put it: "I cannot remember her ever telling me what her life as a child was like. Nor would she tell her grandchildren when I would ask direct and/or indirect questions."[469] Maybe it was because, sadly, no matter how Elise carried herself in public, her private life was "tragic, unhappy, [and] with little" to help her transcend the difficulties she faced in her past, which is Patricia's theory.[470]

Elise died from a stroke at her home in the Edgewater Apartments in Seattle on March 3, 1979. Her remains were cremated. There is no headstone or memorial plaque. Her death was simply noted in The Seattle Times on March 9, 1979, as one of several of those who died the prior week: "Elise Swisher, March 3, 1979."[471] There was no memorial service.

Appropriately enough, there was no obituary to close the last chapter on the book of her life.

APPENDIX I

ROY OLMSTED'S FAMILY HISTORY

Roy's direct lineage can be traced back to the late 1500s in England. It wasn't hard. Someone had already done the work. Indeed, there is a book, meticulously researched and first printed in 1912: *Genealogy of the Olmsted family in America : Embracing the Descendants of James and Richard Olmsted and Covering a Period of Nearly Three Centuries, 1632-1912*, compiled by Henry King Olmsted; revised and completed by Geo. K. Ward. Roy's direct line is set out at the end of this section with reference to the page and individual's assigned number. Tracing forward to Roy likewise was easy using Ancestry.com to compile a family tree from public records.

Roy's seven times great-grandfather, Richard Olmsted II, was the first to arrive in the New World in Boston in 1632.[472] Richard was born in Essex, England, in 1612, and embarked for the New World at 20 years old with his uncle, James Olmsted and other relatives, on the ship "Lion." For a frame of reference, the Mayflower landed in the New World just 12 years before in 1620.

The family were Puritans. They settled first at Mount Wollaston, now Quincy, near Boston, but in the course of the year, "they removed to New Town, now Cambridge, where James

Olmsted had his house lot on the northerly side of Harvard St., upon or near the spot occupied by what has long been known as the "President's House," now called the Wadsworth House. This was the second piece of land acquired by Harvard College.[473]

The Olmsteds became followers of Thomas Hooker, a Puritan minister who came to Massachusetts in 1633 to escape religious persecution in England. Hooker became the first minister of the church at Newtown (again, now known as Cambridge). In 1636, Hooker and about 100 people from his congregation, including the Olmsteds, left Massachusetts and traveled to Connecticut where they started a new settlement. That settlement came to be known as the city of Hartford.

There, the Olmsted name is inscribed on the Founders Monument in Hartford today. There is a <u>Society of the Descendents of the Founders of the City of Hartford</u> that recognizes four Olmsteds as among the founders group James Olmsted, Dr. John Olmsted, Capt. Richard Olmsted and Nicholas Olmsted.[474]

Richard was a soldier in the Pequot Indian War, enlisting in May 1637. He was a magistrate for the Colony of Connecticut in 1658 and held many other colonial offices. It was said that "he had the confidence of the Colony and his townsmen to a high degree."[475] Richard and Elizabeth Haugh were married about 1640 in Hartford and soon thereafter he had Roy's 6x great-grandfather, John Olmsted, in 1649, in Hartford.

Richard and his family moved to and incorporated the town of Norwalk in 1650. John was about a year old. When John grew up, he served in the militia as a Lieutenant. Like his father, he was an important man in the growing town of Norwalk and in 1699 he was chosen Selectman, and again in 1703. John and his wife Mary Benedict had a son, Daniel, in 1685.

Daniel became one of the founders of the town of Ridgefield, CT. Daniel was for many years an influential man in town affairs. In 1732, he was confirmed by the General Assembly, Ensign of the Ridgefield Train Band, which is to say, a company of militia. He was a Representative in 1742 and 1743.[476]

He married Hannah Ketchum, and they had nine children, but it is his second son, Samuel, who is in Roy's direct line. Samuel (1715-1788) was a Representative in the General Court, at various times, for thirty years. He married Abiah Smith in 1737, and they had seven children. Their son Ebenezer (1748-1801) is the one in Roy's direct line and perhaps being the most interesting of his lineage.

It seems that Ebenezer was every bit a rogue. He enlisted in the Connecticut militia on January 24, 1775. He fought throughout the New York Campaign of 1776 at the battles of Long Island, Harlem Heights and White Plains. He joined the 5th Connecticut Continentals on January 1, 1777, as a Lieutenant and fought on his home ground during the British raid on Ridgefield in April 1777. He was wounded during the battle of Germantown on October 4, 1777.

In January 1779, he was encamped at Redding, eight miles from where a young woman named Esther Ingersoll lived with her parents. He took leave and married her on January 17th. Of the marriage, a descendant of Ebenezer has written: "True, it appears he sired my direct ancestor with the minister's daughter a year before they were legally married, but after all, he did finally make an honest woman of her."[477]

After the Revolutionary War ended,[478] Ebenezer settled down to make an honest living and on December 21, 1780, the town of Ridgefield, Connecticut, appointed him constable ""to collect the state tax for the year ensuing." It turns out that Ebenezer was much better "at collecting taxes, was much worse at forwarding them along to Hartford, and appears to have robbed the town blind."[479]

On April 10, 1786, The Town Meeting agreed to "accept the resignation of Lt. Ebenezer Olmsted of his office of collector of ye state taxes on ye list of 1780, on conditions of his accounting with and paying to the Select Men the full that he has collected." And on Sept. 30, 1786 – "Ebenezer Olmsted, late collector of ye state taxes for ye town of Ridgefield, holden under arrest at the town of said Ridgefield, shall be liberated and discharged from said suit, upon condition for the said Olmsted shall fully vest the right" to his property holdings in town. The property includes his 13-acre homestead on Main Street, about 25 acres scattered around town, eight tons of hay, his right to some cows, and "2,258 Continental Dollars." He was ordered to deliver all the foregoing to the town treasurer and told to post a 1,000-pound bond to guarantee payment of the owed taxes.

On March 12, 1787, the town held a sale of the Ebenezer's property. The house fetched only 129 pounds – Olmsted had paid 300 pounds for it in 1782. The sale and confiscations were not enough to cover what was owed to the state, however, and the issue dragged on.

He remained in the community notwithstanding his embarrassment. In 1800, the year before his death, the Congregational Church records that Ebenezer Olmsted still was assigned to the 4th pew. Between 1780 and 1801 when he died, Ebenezer and Esther Ingersoll had at least 12 children. Ebenezer's son Henry was born in Ridgefield in 1784 and is Roy's direct ancestor.

Henry married Sarah Sally Merritt, and their son Oscar Oliver Merritt Olmsted was born in 1816. Apparently, Henry was a Shaker-Quaker.[480] Oscar married Electa Hunt in 1837, and the family, including his father Henry, moved to Prophetstown,[481] Illinois. Both Henry and Oscar were listed as farmers in the 1850 census. This is the start of the westward migration of the Olmsted family.

Oscar's middle son, John Wesley Olmsted, was born in Prophetstown in 1846 and was Roy's father. John Wesley also was a farmer. He married Sarah Rose in 1879 and moved west to Nebraska where their first child, Florence, was born in 1880. Five children followed: Frank (1881); Ralph (1883); Sallie (1884); Roy (1886) and Eunice (1888).

Roy's family moved to Seattle in 1904 when Roy was 18 years old. Roy's father established a real estate firm – Olmsted Realty – and his daughter Sallie would join him in the company.

Here is a timeline of Roy's lineage:

Richard	1612-1687
John	1649-1704
Daniel	1685-1749
Samuel	1715-1788
Ebenezer	1748-1801
Henry	1784-1866
Oscar Oliver	1816-1880
John Wesley	1846-1936
Roy	1886-1966

APPENDIX II

Roy's Letter dated May 28, 1931, to Elise
(on Pacific Steamship Company letterhead)

My dearest Elise: up at my usual hour at 6 a.m. after two good nights of restful sleep, feeling as fit as a fiddle, having had my constitutional walk and breakfast. I shall not direct my conversation to you.

The weather has been ideal. Everyone aboard reflects the sea voyager attitude of friendliness and good humor.

One would have thought I were the President of the Company, the way all officials have treated me. The head steward, the Purser, and even the Captain have gone out of their way to make my trip pleasant, to say nothing of the courtesy that has been extended me by those in the lesser capacities. Yesterday afternoon, the Captain introduced himself to me and took me up into the Pilot house, showed me everything concerning the operation of the boat. A very estimable gentleman and said any time I and my family were traveling to be sure and make it known to him. In fact, dear, the boat was mine.

A Mr. Dorigan, owner of the Art Craft Dyeworks in Seattle made himself known to me and asked for the privilege of sharing my stateroom, which I arranged for him through the Purser at no additional expense. He is a very nice gentleman and enjoyable traveling companion.

Well that will do for now about the trip and myself. I now am inquiring about you. It was not so easy in leaving you and Patsy behind, but when you unobtrusively stepped aside to save for the pressing needs, it was in evidence of ever noble character that made me rejoice in my heart at my great good fortune in having such a pal and sweetheart.

There hasn't been a minute when walking or wherever I was that you and Patsy were not in my thoughts.

There will be no more trips alone as far as I am concerned. You and Patsy are going to be my companions. Everyone has been lovely to me, but there is no one that can fill the vacancy created by the absence of you and Patricia.

If the balance of this trip turns out as well as this voyage has, I shall return to you with very joyous news. I am very hopeful. The old fog horn is blasting as we are approaching Golden Gate. In an other [sic] hour the boat will be docked, and I on my way for a ticket to Merced.

Remember me to Milli, Gladys, and any one who inquires.

PS. I met a Mrs. Arlnett, supposed to be somebody of consequence on GA.

Henry Dorigan insists that you, Patsy and I shall come to his home in Mercer Island for the weekend as soon as he returns. You will like him very much.

Hope your cold is better and that you are in the pink. Smile - my thoughts you know. Kiss and hug Patsy [?] for me and tell her that her secretary will take good care of her business upon return.

Remember me also to Berth and Jack. I will write them from Merced.

Lots of love and kisses your ever loving Roy.

ACKNOWLEDGEMENTS

There are a lot of people to thank for their help along the way in researching and writing this book, but first and foremost, I have to acknowledge and thank Patricia McFarlane, Elise's daughter. She took my first phone call and shared her memories with me freely and with good humor. I knew that I had hit the jackpot when she precisely recalled her Aunt Lily's address in Philadelphia when, as a teenager in the late 1930s, she traveled alone from Seattle by train across the country to meet her aunt for the first time. She is a delightful woman and I am grateful for the memories she shared with me.

Patricia's three sons likewise were immensely helpful. John and Mark McFarlane especially deserve my gratitude. John's enthusiasm for his family's history and his willingness to meet with me and answer my endless questions set the tone for this project. John, his wife Cathy and two daughters, treated me like family rather than the prying interloper I felt to be at times.

And then there was Mark, the magician. He is my hero for keeping Elise's keepsakes when his mother no longer could hold them. He continually surprised me, finding new documents or photos in the two storage boxes of Elise's things. He and John spent an entire day with me going through the boxes and scanning photos, sharing stories and letting me dig through the materials at will.

I met Elise's third grandson, Steve, late in the project. He listened to me for two hours one Saturday morning and gave me some more great insights into Elise. It was Steve's daughter, Katie, who took my first call, then managed a video chat with me, and connected me with the rest of her family. Without that link, I would not have had the good fortune of getting to know the family, nor would I have been able to interview Patricia.

I hope this journey was as much fun for the McFarlane family as it was for me.

Finding the descendants of Elise's sister, Lily, was one of the great discoveries along the way for me. I learned that Lily's daughter was named Elise; Lily's granddaughter was named Elise; and, one of her daughters likewise was named Elise! Early on, Lily's granddaughter sent me a photo of a portrait of Elise that I had not seen before as well as the photo of the Parsche family. It raised my hopes that there might be a few more relics still around and did I get lucky. Sharing those two photos with John McFarlane led to him showing me the original portrait and ultimately to Mark's two boxes!

I was also able to find the descendants of Elise's half-sister, Julia, who live in England. I hope they enjoyed learning more about Elise in America as much as I enjoyed learning about the first Parsche family in England.

When I started this project, I reached out to Brad Holden, author, historian and self-described Finder of Old Things! Brad had just published *Seattle Prohibition: Bootleggers, Rumrunners & Graft in the Queen City* and I contacted him to ask for advice on researching Elise. He was so generous with help, encouragement and advice, including putting me in contact with Katie McFarlane in the first place. Brad also connected me with two others who also were doing research into Elise – Rebecca Demerast and McCall Gordon – each of whom gladly spent time discussing the elusive Elise with me.

Allee Monheim, Public Service Librarian, Special Collections, University of Washington, answered endless questions and always had a reference or pointer for me. The staff at the Seattle Public Library and at the National Archives, Pacific Region, likewise were always helpful. These are the unsung heroes of historical research.

Special thanks to Anna Elam, Library Collections Manager, Museum of History and Industry ("MOHAI").

Friends along the way, especially my dear friends Ellen, Nina, and KT, had great input for me, recognizing a good story when they heard it, and encouraging me to write it.

And the most thanks to my wife, Pam, who gave me the time, most of the time, to research and write this book, and to whom it would be dedicated if we both didn't revere the wisdom and knowledge of the elders in our lives like Patricia who is a treasure.

Finally, any mistakes in the book are my own.

BIBLIOGRAPHY

The best historical sources for Elise's story, Roy's story, and Prohibition in Seattle are the newspapers of the time. The Seattle Daily Times, the Seattle Daily News, and The Star each provide a different emphasis and viewpoint of the daily drama. The digital versions are available online through various platforms, including the Seattle Public Library. The demise of the print version Seattle Post-Intelligencer in 2009 led to the digitization of the archives. Unfortunately for the period covered in this book, some of the digital copies were poorly copied and are unreadable.

Although not traditionally considered a bibliographic resource, online genealogy platforms like Ancestry.com provide access to billions of historical records, articles, and various databases. For example, building the Olmsted family tree resulted in the discovery of stories, photos, and records shared by the many descendants of Roy Olmsted's family line.

Norman H. Clark, The Dry Years: Prohibition and Social Change in Washington (Seattle: University of Washington Press, 1988).

Norman H. Clark, *Roy Olmstead, a Rumrunning King on Puget Sound,* The Pacific Northwest Quarterly, Jul., 1963, Vol. 54, No. 3 (July 1963).

Ross Cunningham. "Aunt Vivian and the King of the Rum Runners: Historical Vignettes," December 18, 1977, A-12; (Seattle Times).

Samuel Dash, Richard F. Schwartz and Robert E. Knowlton, The Eavesdroppers, Rutgers University Press, New Jersey (1959).

Brian Hochman, The Listeners: A History of Wiretapping in the United States, Harvard University Press (2022).

Brad Holden, Bootleggers, Rumrunners & Graft in the Queen City, Arcadia Publishing (2019).

Brad Holden, Seattle Mystic: Alfred M. Hubbard, Inventor, Bootlegger and Psychedelic Pioneer, Arcadia Publishing (2021).

Philip Metcalfe, Whispering Wires: The Tragic Tale of an American Bootlegger" (Inkwater Press (2007).

Walter F. Murphy, Wiretapping on Trial: A Case Study in the Judicial Process, (Random House 1965).

Ralph Bushnell Potts, Seattle Heritage, Superior Publishing Co., Seattle, Washington (1955).

ENDNOTES

[1] Lily named her daughter Elise, who in turn named her daughter Elise, who in turn named her daughter Elise, carrying on the tradition.

[2] Patricia's recollections come from her correspondence with author Philip Metcalfe in 1993-94, as part of his research for his book *Whispering Wires: The Tragic Tale of an American Bootlegger,* Inkwater Press (2007). [hereinafter, "Metcalfe Letters"] Metcalfe Letters, July 12, 1993.

[3] Metcalfe Letters, July 12, 1993.

[4] Elise did save some things from later in her life after her marriage to Roy. These materials were passed down to Patricia upon Elise's death, and are now preserved by Patricia's children. These items are referred to throughout the book as the "Olmsted Collection," and a copy of the materials are on file with the author.

One observation: how important any of these things were to Elise cannot be proven today, nor can it be said with certainty that these were the only documents and things saved by her over her lifetime. Some things may have been disposed of at her death, lost over time, or given away. It is important not to overstate the significance of any item in the Olmsted Collection. At the same time, these items were part of Elise's life and saved by her. They tell us something about her interests, character and personality.

5 To avoid confusion over her name, if that's possible, "Elise," the name she adopted and that first appears in her marriage certificate with Roy, is used throughout the book except when "Elsie" is used as part of a quotation or document.

6 See the following link for the story of the family business and its success: https://cutglass.org/articles/art144.htm

7 The age of indenture in the merchant navy was thirteen under the Merchant Shipping Act. Christian would later emigrate to Canada and assume the name Harry Patterson.

8 1891 England Census.

9 Hermann married Theresa Westrick in 1892. She was born in Germany in about 1870. They had two children, Theresa (1893) and Minnie (1894). Hermann died in 1896 at age 30. Theresa remarried Adam Wittekind in August 1897 and had four more children, passing away in England in 1952.

10 1891 England Census.

11 1901 EnglandCensus.

12 1901 England Census.

13 1911 Census of England and Wales.

14 From the Liverpool Echo.

15 The Guardian, May 13, 1913.

16 Converting to dollars in 1915 is not straightforward but if 20 shillings equaled 1 pound, and 1 pound in 1915 equaled about $4.75, then Lily would have received about $20 per month. See https://www.measuringworth.com/calculators/exchange/ A factory worker's wages in England at that time would have been almost triple the amount.

17 The granddaughter of Elise's sister Lily kindly shared this family memory in an Interview for this book.

18 The Seattle Star, at 1, 4 (Nov. 21, 1924); see also The Bakersfield Calfornian at p. 3 (Dec. 1, 1924).

19 Olmsted Collection. Sir Aukland Geddes' papers are at the Churchill Center in England. There is no copy of a personal letter to Elise thanking her for her services.

20 Metcalfe Letters, May 28, 1993.

21 Metcalfe, at 68-70.

22 Interview with John McFarlane dated 12 May 2024.

23 MI5 records show they apprehended at least 65 German spies throughout the War, though some estimates suggest the number may have been higher *See* MI5 in World War I at https://www.mi5.gov.uk/history/mi5s-early-years/world-war-i

24 As noted later in this book, in the Fall of 1942, Elise went to work for the War Department as a clerk in the Overseas Supply Division, Operations Branch, in the Seattle Port of

Embarkation. The Port was established in January 1942 and became one of the busiest embarkation points for the Pacific theater during the War, critical for moving troops and supplies overseas. See https://www.historylink.org/File/10986. Perhaps it was Elise's security badge for access to the Port that her grandson saw, not an OSS badge.

25 Metcalfe, at 69.

26 The actual identity of the father of Elise's child cannot be confirmed through Patricia's DNA and available records in British Columbia or military records and ship manifests do not solve the puzzle.

27 For the story, see https://flemingsderbytownship.ca/2018/03/12/r-m-s-tunisian-montreal-to-liverpool-june-27-to-july-6-1903/

28 In her denial of the government's abandonment claim, Elise said that she traveled in Canada for a year after her arrival in 1919. See The Seattle Star, November 21, 1924, at 1. It is possible that she stayed in Montreal until she had the baby and then completed the journey to Vancouver with the child. It seems improbable because it would have been a much harder journey with a child in hand and there are no records to support the theory. However, knowing Elise's fortitude, one can imagine her showing up in Vancouver with a child, searching for the father who either can't be found or rejects that the child is his own, and then Elise deciding to give the child up for adoption. Whatever

is true, it had to be emotionally overwhelming and frightening for a young girl of nineteen.

[29] The Seattle Star, at 1 (Nov. 21, 1924).

[30] As noted, his DNA test is unrelated to this book. We do not know why he took a test or whether he has even reviewed the results or knows that Patricia, a close match, is in fact his aunt. While he ultimately may see Patricia's DNA result and inquire, he has not been contacted by Patricia or her family at this time.

[31] Immigration Act of 1917, 39 Stat. 874. Section 2 of the Act imposed a tax of $8 on every alien entering the country but excluded aliens who resided in Canada, for example, for one year prior to entry.

[32] Immigration Form dated Nov. 13, 1920.

[33] See Enumeration District 0191 for Seattle, available through SteveMorris.org. None of the B. Cunningham's that appear in the 1920 census live on Summit Ave., or have any apparent connection to Elise.

[34] Alien Certificates were issued to immigrants upon payment of the required "head tax", or immigration fee, at Vancouver and Victoria, British Columbia, surrendered at Seattle, Washington, between 1917 and 1924. These Alien Certificates served as permits to enter the United States from foreign contiguous territory. As noted, all alien persons entering the United States across contiguous borders were required to submit to an examination prior to entry and those intending to remain permanently were

required to pay the head tax, which, according to the Certificate of Arrival, she paid.

35 See List or Manifest of Alien Passengers Applying for Admission to the United States from Foreign Contiguous Territory,

36 The Seattle Star, November 21, 1924, at 4.

37 The Form may have been corrected by hand to indicate yes to a prior entry, but it is unclear due to the quality of the copy.

38 The Albany Rooms is now The Regal Hotel in Vancouver. It was essentially a Single Room Occupancy building. See https://www.heritagesitefinder.ca/location/1044-1048-granville-st-vancouver-bc

39 Professor Norman Clark says that Roy met Elise in Vancouver. Clark interviewed Roy a number of times between 1958 to 1960 for his 1963 article "Roy Olmstead, A Rumrunning King on Puget Sound," so it may have been something Roy told him. Clark, at 91. The shame of it is that Clark's papers are nowhere to be found. Nor are there any notes of Clark's purported interview with Elise, which apparently took place in 1966 for Clark's later book *The Dry Years*. Philip Metcalf repeats the story of where they met verbatim in his *Whispering Wires* book without any citation, but probably relied on Clark. Metcalfe, at 68-70.

40 Metcalfe, at 64.

41 Seattle Post-Intelligencer, Nov. 19, 1924, at 6.

42 Seattle Post-Intelligencer, Nov. 19, 1924, at 6.

43 Seattle Daily Times, June 14, 1922, at 3. The Seattle Daily Times headline read "Ex Police Lieutenant Arrested. Roy Olmsted Accused as Runner." To add insult to injury, it was also reported that Roy was arrested on a charge of speeding at 30 mph on Eastlake Avenue.

44 Seattle Daily Times, July 7, 1922, at 1, 4.

45 The Seattle Star, July 8, 1922, at 5.

46 Seattle Post-Intelligencer, Nov. 19, 1924, at 6.

47 Seattle Daily Times, Jan. 28,1926, at 1. Whitney's statement was made under oath at the Whispering Wires trial. It appears that Elise may not have had contact with Whitney before June 1922 while working undercover. Lyle may have embellished his story of Elise's regular meetings with agents, or she may have only dealt with field agents at the time. The absence of any records of her informant days leaves the timing largely to speculation.

48 Metcalfe, at 69.

49 Metcalfe, at 5.

50 Metcalfe, at 5.

51 Roy's colorful family genealogy and history of his direct lineage is set out in Appendix I.

52 Metcalfe, at 4-5.

---

53 Metcalfe letters, May 8, 1993. Apparently, Roy's mother, Sarah, wrote a letter of reconciliation but for whatever reason, she didn't send it. After Cottie's death in 1959, Sarah's daughters gave the letter to Roy. Sarah had hidden it, but not destroyed it.

54 Seattle Daily Times, April 7, 1909, at 5.

55 Racial slurs such as this one were common in the newspapers and otherwise in that era. Because it and other references are part of a quote, they are retained here.

56 The Seattle Star, Nov. 20, 1914, at 1.

57 The book was titled "Border Play; or, From Broadway to the Rio Grande."

58 By way of explanation, Roy would appear in court at sentencing and the judges often deferred to his recommendations. He soon figured out that he could sell his favorable recommendation to a defendant.

59 Clark, at 90.

60 Metcalfe, at 7.

61 Metcalfe, at 7.

62 Seattle Daily Times, March 22, 1920, at 1, 5.

63 Seattle Daily Times, June 8, 1920, at 1.

64 Metcalfe, at 8.

65 Clark, Norman H., *Roy Olmstead, a Rumrunning King on Puget Sound,* 54 The Pacific Northwest Quarterly (July 1963), No. 3 at. 89.

[66] Seattle Daily Times, June 14, 1922, at 3. The Seattle Daily Times headline read "Ex Police Lieutenant Arrested. Roy Olmsted Accused as Runner." To add insult to injury, it was also reported that Roy was arrested on a charge of speeding at 30 mph on Eastlake Avenue.

[67] Metcalfe Letters, May 28, 1993.

[68] Metcalfe Letters, May 28, 1993.

[69] Metcalfe letters, June 11, 1993.

[70] Seattle Daily Times, February 2, 1924, at 4.

[71] Metcalfe, at 16. Elise's daughter Patricia is the source of Metcalfe's story. Patricia says the girls "felt involved and a part of the operation....they felt it was a family thing which was taken away from them by the divorce. They were angry at their mother and inclined to blame her." Metcalfe Letters, May 28, 1993.

[72] Professor Clark either made a mistake in asserting that Cottie was the informant, or he got hoodwinked during the research for his book by Roy. Clark says the story that Elise was the informant "grew out of testimony offered during the trial of 1925-26 that Mrs. Olmstead had for a while in 1922 assisted the federal agents – but the reference was to the rumrunner's first wife, not to Elsie. The footnote cites to the Bill of Exceptions in the Ninth Circuit and to a newspaper article titled "Mrs. Olmstead in Blue" in the Seattle Post-Intelligencer on Jan. 20, 1926. Neither support the statement in any way. Metcalfe adds to the story, writing that "probably after the last of her

loud disagreements with Roy" Cottie appeared at the Prohibition offices and explained the detailed workings of Roy's operations, including turning over the keys to his safety deposit box. Metcalfe at 16-17. But as Commissioner Lyle stated, it was Elise that met with the Prohibition agents regularly and Whitney who said that Elise told him that she gave Lyle the safety deposit box keys. Clark had interviewed Roy several times, and it is conceivable that Roy tried to protect Elise as he always did even after the divorce by shifting the informant blame to Cottie, but as noted, Clark's papers and notes of any interviews have disappeared. But the evidence is overwhelming that Elise was in fact the informant.

[73] The Seattle Star, June 8, 1926, at 1.

[74] The Seattle Star, June 8, 1926, at 1.

[75] The Seattle Star, June 8, 1926, at 1.

[76] The Seattle Star, June 8, 1926, at 1.

[77] The Seattle Star, June 8, 1926, at 1.

[78] The Seattle Star, June 8, 1926, at 1.

[79] Metcalfe Letters, May 28, 1993.

[80] Vivienne's high school yearbook is online and available through Ancestry.com.

[81] Los Angeles Times, July 4, 1926, at 31.

[82] Metcalfe, at 70.

[83] Seattle Post-Intelligencer, January 23, 1926, at 1.

84 Metcalfe, at 64.

85 Seattle Post-Intelligencer, Nov 2, 1924, at 33.

86 Olmsted Collection.

87 One example involves Al Hubbard, the man who betrayed Roy to Prohibition agents, after all that Roy had done for Hubbard. After all the lies and betrayal became public, Hubbard and Roy chanced to meet in the U.S. Marshal's office in November 1927 as the third prosecution of Roy was getting underway. Hubbard and Roy shook hands while agents in the office "looked on in amazement at the obvious emotional warmth that still existed between a wealthy bootlegger and his youthful betrayer." Metcalfe, at 274.

88 Seattle Daily Times, March 16, 1926, at 10.

89 Seattle Daily Times, March 16, 1926, at 10.

90 Olmsted Collection. Two copies of the nicely bound appraisal were among the few things Elise saved. Along with photographs of the home and its furnishings, it is almost as if Elise wanted to keep it as a record of the things she once possessed.

91 From an advertisement in 1922, available here https://www.ebay.com/itm/155138513917.

92 Some of the photographs of the house and Elise from a photo shoot in the Fall of 1924 are included in this book. The photographs are retained in the Olmsted Collection by the McFarlane family.

[93] The Seattle Star, June 6, 1924, at 2; Metcalfe, at 29-32.

[94] Seattle Daily Times, June 3, 1924, at 11.

[95] Metcalfe, at 33.

[96] The construction of the boat had caused quite a stir and the newspapers had a time with the story. A reporter for The Seattle Star went down to the drydocks and tried to charter the boat for a fishing trip. The story is quite humorous with the reporter getting someone working on the boat to agree that the boat could hold quite a few cases… of fish. The Seattle Star, June 12, 1924, at 12. There is also a sketch of the craft with the article and a note that the vessel had been painted all black, which obviously was for one purpose and it is not aesthetics.

[97] Metcalfe, at 33.

[98] Metcalfe, at 96.

[99] Seattle Daily Times, Nov. 29, 1924, at 5. A full report on the operations of the *Elsie* was made by Coast Guard Capt. F. G. Dodge.

[100] Metcalfe. at 96.

[101] Seattle Daily Times, February 4, 1923, at 7.

[102] Seattle Daily Times, September 13, 1923.

[103] Seattle Post-Intelligencer, October 31, 1924, at 11. The injured worker was represented in the action by George Vandeveer who later would represent Roy and Elise and many of the other defendants in the Whispering Wires trial. For now, in response to claims that the boat

belonged to Graignic, Vandeveer said "when the time comes, I will prove by documentary evidence that the *Elsie* was built with Roy Olmsted's money and was his boat."

104 Seattle Daily Times, September 28, 1924, at 28; Metcalfe at 96.

105 Metcalfe, at 96.

106 Metcalfe, at 97; Olmsted Collection. The correspondence between Dow and the insurer was among the papers that Elise saved. They provide some reading entertainment in the form of legal jousting between Dow and the insurance company.

107 *See* Brad Holden, *Seattle Mystic: Alfred M. Hubbard, Inventor, Bootlegger and Psychedelic Pioneer* (2021).

108 Metcalfe, at 109.

109 Holden, at 31. Holden says that Roy needed convincing by Hubbard and Elise to build the station and that the station had enormous economic potential. That may be true because Elise and Hubbard certainly were enthusiastic about radio. But overall, Roy was way ahead on the use of radio to communicate with his ships and airplanes and was a radio bug himself. It probably didn't take much to convince him.

110 Seattle Post-Intelligencer, 11 July 1924, at 15.

111 Seattle Post-Intelligencer, 11 July 1924, at 15.

112 Metcalfe, at 109.

[113] Olmsted Collection. The original license grant was for three months.

[114] Seattle Daily Times, April 4, 1925, at 9.

[115] Seattle Daily Times, April 4, 1925, at 9.

[116] Metcalfe, at 101-102. The source of this story in Metcalfe's book is unknown and undocumented. It all or some may be true but the documentation for it is lacking. Lyle was quoted in a newspaper report shortly after the raid on the Olmsted home as saying that Roy "operates a fast fleet of rum ships, augmented by motor cars, motorcycles and trucks, **radio and possibly airplanes**, and includes an army of men and women." Seattle Post Intelligencer, November 11, 1924, at 9 (emphasis added).

[117] The Seattle Star, May 15, 1926, at 2.

[118] Seattle Daily Times, October 22, 1924, at 21.

[119] Metcalfe, at 102.

[120] KFQX was not Seattle's first licensed radio station, however. Station KJR was the first, licensed on August 21, 1921. It was the pioneer station for Seattle. See Schneider, J., *Seattle Radio History: KJR & KOMO* in the Radio Historian (2011), available at: <http://www.theradiohistorian.org/Seattle/kjr%20komo%20history.htm>.

[121] Metcalfe, at 102.

[122] The Butler Hotel was one of the leading Seattle hotels in 1924 and was located on the corner of Second and James

St. During Prohibition, the Butler Hotel's Rose Room was known for serving liquor and often cited until it closed in 1933. "The waiters served ice and ginger ale. Bellboys produced the bourbon, Scotch or gin - or good wines. Naturally, the pretense was common knowledge, a tolerance typical of that Seattle era. *See* https://pauldorpat.com/2017/01/21/seattle-now-then-the-butler-did-it/ quoting Ross Cunningham, Seattle Times, July 15, 1977.

[123] Metcalfe, at 103.

[124] Metcalfe, at 103.

[125] The Seattle Star, November 18, 1924, at 1.

[126] Olmsted Collection. Copies are on file with the author.

[127] Olmsted Collection. About three dozen pictures from a professional photo shoot of Elise and her home were among the items kept by Elise. These never-before-seen images show the glamor and wealth Roy and Elise enjoyed. They were probably taken in the Fall of 1924, perhaps spurred by the Radio Digest request for photos. They are a window into Elise's life that would close forever after the government raid at the end of November 1924.

[128] Radio Digest Letter to Miss Vivien Potter, November 20, 1924. Note the spelling of the first name, perhaps intentionally gender ambiguity by Elise.

[129] See HistoryLink, Peter Blecha, *Pioneering Seattle radio station KJR jumps from 500 to 1,000 watts of power on January 21, 1925*, posted April 13, 2022. <https://www.historylink.org/file/22457>

[130] Indeed, in an article about Roy's bootlegging, the Washington Secretary of State website currently and definitively states that Elise's children's radio show contained coded messages:

Elise Olmstead, Roy's wife, started KFQX radio, the first station in Seattle, based out of their mansion. Her most popular program was a kid's bedtime story show called "Aunt Vivian" during which Elise slipped in coded messages to the launches in transit on Puget Sound.

https://www.sos.wa.gov/es/about-office/from-our-corner/5926/History%20Friday%3A%20The%20King%20of%20Puget%20Sound%20Bootleggers

[131] Seattle Daily Times, November 22, 1924, at 5.

[132] Seattle Daily Times, November 22, 1924, at 6. If Lyle and his agents did record all the broadcasts, there is no record of those recordings. How were the broadcasts recorded? Recording, unlike radio, wasn't new technology per se. In 1877, Thomas Edison heard "Mary had a little lamb" emanate from a machine into which he had just spoken the ditty. It was the first time a recording of the human voice had been reproduced, and the event signaled the birth of the phonograph. If Lyle and the prohibition

office possessed recording equipment, and made
recordings of Aunt Vivian's broadcasts, it is lost to history.

[133] The radio idea however would resurface a few years later
during the Whitney graft trial when Hubbard testified that
"Whitney thought it would be a good idea to be able to
get in touch with Olmstead and the boats. So we decided
to put the station on the fifth floor, over the prohibition
office, presumably for prohibition work, but really to tip
off the boats about the Coast Guard." The claim was
preposterous, and Whitney was acquitted,

[134] Rebecca Demarest interview with Patricia McFarlane,
August 2020.

[135] Metcalfe, at 149. The decline of the radio business and
Hubbard's standing in the radio community may have
been the turning point for him. Nine months after the
raid, Hubbard met with Whitney and brokered a deal to
become an informant.

[136] *See* Pioneering Seattle radio station KJR jumps from 500 to
1,000 watts of power on January 21, 1925, at
<http://www.theradiohistorian.org/Seattle/kjr%20komo%
20history.htm>.

[137] The Olmsted Collection. The saga of Olmsted's ultimate
disposition of the station is a long story ending with Fisher
successfully suing Roy and others in the Fall of 1926.
Fisher ultimately paid Roy $10,000, which Roy later said
went into Hubbard's pocket. One of the documents that
Elise kept was the 8-page affidavit of Birt Fisher in support

of his injunctive relief case. It chronicles Roy's every effort to wring any money possible out of the sale of the station and its equipment and to avoid paying the station's debts. What Elise must have felt is not documented anywhere.

[138] Metcalfe, at 105.

[139] Metcalfe, at 105.

[140] Metcalfe, at 106.

[141] Seattle Post Intelligencer, November 25, 1924, at 3.

[142] Metcalfe, at 107.

[143] Metcalfe, at 108.

[144] Metcalfe, at 108. Mrs. Whitney's role in the entire investigation was so improper that today, it likely would have been enough to quash any charges. She was not an agent. She had no formal investigative role. Not only did she attend the raid, but she also reviewed, revised, organized and prepared the transcripts of the wiretaps. Then she disposed of the agents' original notes taken at the time of the intercept.

[145] Seattle Daily Time, November 19, 1924, at 1.

[146] Seattle Daily Time, November 19, 1924, at 1.

[147] Seattle Daily Time, November 19, 1924, at 1.

[148] Seattle Daily Time, November 19, 1924, at 4.

[149] Seattle Daily Time, November 19, 1924, at 4.

[150] Seattle Post-Intelligencer, November 19, 1924, at 6.. The "Potter" residence was wiretapped at the end of July 1924.

According to Metcalfe, wires ran from a telephone pole on the side of the house, across an alley and into the basement of a neighbor's house. Metcalfe, at 70.

[151] Seattle Post-Intelligencer, November 19, 1924, at 6.

[152] Roy was careful about what he said on the phone after he learned about the wiretapping. But he couldn't help himself to have fun at the government expense with it. He set up an elaborate practical joke to draw Whitney and his agents to a garage to make a supposed seizure of a large load. When Whitney arrived, catching Roy and his colleagues in the garage, they burst out laughing because the garage was clean. Roy joked with Whitney: "Tell me Bill, how did you get this tip?" They continued to joke that Whitney should have waited half an hour and must have got the time wrong from his source. Roy suggested that they all go downtown and have breakfast together, and then he leaked the story of the fruitless raid to the press, including the invitation to breakfast. Metcalfe, at 80-82.

[153] Metcalfe, at 70-71. McKinney ultimately would be discovered and prosecuted in 1930 along with Lyle, Whitney, Corwin, and Fryant.

[154] Seattle Post Intelligencer, November 19, 1924, at 6.

[155] Seattle Post Intelligencer, November 19, 1924, at 6.

[156] Seattle Post Intelligencer, November 19, 1924, at 6.

157 See e.g., The Bakersfield Californian, December 1, 1924, at
3 ("Woman Trailing Bootleg Suspect Becomes His
Wife"); The Knoxville News, December 4, 1924, at 1
("She Made a Poor Booze Sleuth, but a Loyal Wife").

158 Seattle Post Intelligencer, November 19, 1924 at 1.

159 The Seattle Star, November 21, 1924, at 4. It is also possible
that Elise went back in July and returned later, but no
further immigration records under her various aliases used
at the time have been found.

160 Despite the reference to the date of Elise's entry in this news
article, there is no record of her entry in October 1920
under any of her names - Parsche, Parche, Potter, or
Campbell. She did enter in November 1920 and again in
July 1921.

161 Seattle Post Intelligencer, November 21, 1924 at 1. The
story also was reported in Vancouver, British Columbia,
but without any additional information about Elise or her
time in Vancouver. The Vancouver Sun, November 21,
1924 at 1.

162 The Seattle Star, November 21, 1924, at 1.

163 More speculation but if pushed to give a best guess, it seems
Ruth Elbro was the likely tipster. She and Elise were very
close friends. Ruth lived in the mansion for a time with
Elise and Roy. There are photographs in the Olmsted
Collection of Ruth, one of which is included in this book.
But Ruth turned on Elise and testified against her in the
trial, most likely to secure the chance for her now husband

Dick Elbro to avoid charges and have the chance to re-enter the U.S. from Canada and obtain citizenship. Their friendship may have ceased when the "tip" was published because Elise may have only told Ruth about the child. Elise would have known the source of the tip could only be Ruth. Again, no one knows and there are no records to confirm it one way or the other. It is a best guess only. Whatever the case, Elise learned a valuable lesson about confiding secrets in others.

[164] Metcalfe Letters, May 28, 1993.

[165] Their daughter Patrica was born on July 8, 1925. A simple one sentence announcement of her birth appeared in the newspaper. See Seattle Daily Times, July 16, 1925, at 17.

[166] The Seattle Star, November 18, 1924, at 1.

[167] The Seattle Star, November 18, 1924, at 1.

[168] Elise was the daughter of a successful butcher. It is conceivable that in her childhood, her parents took her on a trip to Italy and perhaps to Germany to see relatives. That she would have done so on her own is belied by her age - her teen years were spent in the midst of World War I. She was but 15 when her mother died and 10 when her father passed. It is unlikely that the family had the funds to make such a trip, and she certainly could not have traveled alone through Europe as a young girl.

[169] Seattle Post-Intelligencer, January 15, 1925, at 3. The caption doesn't say that Elise cooked the cake. Her daughter Patricia said that Elise was not a cook. She tells a

story about Elise trying to make gravy for a dinner, but it separated: "one person got meat drippings, the other got water. This was considered quite funny, and was remembered." Metcalfe Letters, June 11, 1993. But her grandchildren do recall that Elise, later in her life, could cook and bake well enough.

170 Los Angeles Examiner, May 19, 1930, at 4. The comment was made to reporters just prior to her testimony before the 1930 bribery trial of Whitney, Lyle, and McKinney.

171 Seattle Post-Intelligencer, November 25, 1924, at 3.

172 Seattle Post-Intelligencer, November 25, 1924, at 3.

173 Seattle Daily News, November 23, 1924, at 1.

174 Seattle Daily Times, November 23, 1924, at 13.

175 Seattle Daily Times, November 28, 1924, at 1. The government successfully moved to transfer the case to federal court but the temporary restraining order remained in place. Seattle Daily Times, December 5, 1924, at 4. Finch filed a motion in federal court on December 10th to remand the case back to state court, arguing that no federal statute governed the agents' conduct. Seattle Daily Times, December 11, 1924, at 8. Federal District Court Judge Cushman denied the motion on December 20th, thereby keeping the case at the federal level. Seattle Daily Times, December 21, 1924, at 9.

176 Seattle Daily Times, November 28, 1924, at 9. Again, the story of coded bedtime stories consumed Whitney and has

become urban legend. It is remarkable, however, that Elise never expressly denied the allegation in her several affidavits – calling the claim "unjustly" made is hardly a fulsome denial and probably has added to the urban legend's longevity.

[177] Seattle Daily Times, November 30, 1924 at 12.

[178] Seattle Daily Times, December 12, 1924, at 24.

[179] Ultimately, Hubbard dropped the lawsuit when he became a Prohibition agent and betrayed Roy.

[180] Seattle Daily Times, December 29, 1924, at 1.

[181] Seattle Post-Intelligencer, January 9, 1925, at 2.

[182] Seattle Post-Intelligencer, January 9, 1925, at 2.

[183] Seattle Post Intelligencer, November 24, 1924, at 15.

[184] Seattle Daily Times, November 25, 1924, at 4.

[185] Seattle Daily Times, January 30, 1925, at 1. The resolution was sent to Judge Neterer and the Department of Justice. The existence of the resolution was confirmed by the foreman of the grand jury, but the content was not disclosed. A copy of the resolution has not been found.

[186] Seattle Post-Intelligencer, February 18, 1925, at 5.

[187] A plea in abatement is a motion that attacks a technical defect in the pleading but not the right or authority of the government to bring a case. The pleading is available from the National Archives Pacific Alaska Region, Seattle, as

part of the records of federal prosecutions in the district court.

188 The remaining defendants had their own counsel and joined the pleading.

189 The newspapers wanted to know who gave Roy the copy of the wiretap document included in the Plea in Abatement. Indeed, the newspaper made the point well that Roy's network reached into the police force: "That Olmsted had access, thru a sub rosa connection with a man attached to the police organization, to copies of these records was the amazing story that was being circulated in federal building corridors Tuesday." The Seattle Star, April 7, 1925, at 1.

190 Neterer's opinion is reported at 7 F.2d 756 (1925).

191 Seattle Post-Intelligencer, Sept. 13, 1925, at 92.

192 United States v. Olmstead, 7 F.2d 760, 763 (1925). Judge Neterer in fact was wrong because the state of Washington did in fact prohibit wiretapping.

193 For example, Roy opened an account at Commerce Bank under the name Robert Dunbar. The bank's president was a customer. The money from Roy's operations would then be transferred to a Consolidated Exporters account in Vancouver. Metcalfe, at 150.

194 Seattle Daily Times, November 20, 1924, at 5.

195 Seattle Daily Times, November 22, 1924, at 6

196 Metcalfe, at 149.

197 Metcalfe, at 158.

198 Metcalfe, at 160.

199 Seattle Daily Times, November 26, 1925, at 1.

200 Seattle Daily Times, November 26, 1925, at 3.

201 Seattle Daily Times, November 26, 1925, at 2.

202 Henry Leverage wrote the story "Whispering Wires" in the Saturday Evening Post and playwright Late McLaurin produced it as a play on Broadway in 1922 to great acclaim. The play went on tour and arrived in Seattle at the Metropolitan Theater (now site of the Fairmont Olympic Hotel) in April 1924. The show was a hit. The detective story is about a man who receives a blackmail letter, refuses to go along, and later receives a threatening phone call - a death threat whispered over the wires. He is found dead in his locked office later with the audience asking how the deed was done. There is a good chance that the Olmsted case was dubbed the Whispering Wires trial from the plot line of the play.

203 Seattle Daily Times, January 19, 1926, at 1.

204 Hazel MacDonald was among the many reporters covering the opening of the trial. She was a pioneering woman journalist at a time when female correspondents were rare and, later, she would become the first accredited female War correspondent in World War II. She wrote for *Photoplay*, a precursor to the modern-day celebrity magazine, and she also was a screenwriter in Los Angeles before returning to journalism. So she knew a good story when she heard one and found this "new bootleg

aristocracy" to be the stuff of the movies. Seattle Post-Intelligencer, January 22, 1926, at 2.

[205] Seattle Daily Times, January 19, 1926, at 3.

[206] Seattle Post-Intelligencer, January 20, 1926, at 2.

[207] Seattle Post-Intelligencer, January 20, 1926, at 3

[208] There is no complete transcript of the trial proceedings. The court stenographer was Robert R. Brott, and he would produce daily transcripts, but no complete set has been found. Seattle Daily Times, January 21, 1926 at 1. Portions of transcripts marked for assignment of error by the defense upon appeal of Roy's conviction to the U.S. Court of Appeals for the Ninth Circuit can be found in the National Archives. These relate largely to the defense objections at trial over the introduction of the "whispering wires" testimony. None of the testimony related to Elise is included in the index for appeal because, of course, she was acquitted. It is a shame that history has lost the full record of the trial proceedings. Historians and researchers now must rely on newspaper accounts of the trial.

[209] Seattle Post-Intelligencer, January 19, 1926, at 1.

[210] Seattle Post-Intelligencer, January 19, 1926, at 1

[211] Seattle Post-Intelligencer, January 21, 1926, at 1.

[212] Seattle Daily Times, January 21, 1926, at 8.

[213] Seattle Daily Times, January 21, 1926, at 8.

[214] Seattle Post-Intelligencer, January 21, 1926, at 1.

215 Seattle Daily Times, January 21, 1926, at 8.

216 Seattle Post-Intelligencer, January 21, 1926, at 1. There is no verbatim transcript of Revelle's opening statement, only as reported and quoted in the newspapers. Revelle apparently also referred to Elise's "unconventional relationship" with Roy, living with him in the Mount Baker home before they were married. But Judge Neterer would not allow it in evidence later in the trial when Revelle tried to elicit those facts from his first witness, Peter Miller. Seattle Post-Intelligencer, January 23, 1926, at 1. The digital copy of the newspaper unfortunately is not very readable.

217 Seattle Daily Times, January 21, 1926, at 8.

218 Seattle Post-Intelligencer, February 10, 1926, at 2. As an aside, this exchange should put to rest any disagreement over whether Elise or Cottie had been the government informant. Clearly, it was Elise.

219 Seattle Daily Times, January 28, 1926, at 1, 8.

220 Metcalfe, at 187.

221 Seattle Daily Times, January 23, 1926 at 3.

222 Seattle Post-Intelligencer, January 23, 1926, at 1.

223 Seattle Post-Intelligencer, January 23, 1926, at 1.

224 Seattle Post-Intelligencer, January 25, 1926, at 2.

225 Metcalfe, at 189.

226 Metcalfe, at 199-200.

[227] Seattle Post-Intelligencer, June 6, 1924, at 13.

[228] Olmsted Collection. A copy of the photograph is included in this book.

[229] Seattle Daily Times, January 25, 1926, at 1.

[230] Seattle Daily Times, January 25, 1926, at 1.

[231] Seattle Daily Times, January 25, 1926, at 1.

[232] Seattle Post-Intelligencer, January 28, 1926, at 3.

[233] Seattle Post-Intelligencer, January 28, 1926, at 3.

[234] Seattle Post-Intelligencer, January 28, 1926, at 2. The government eventually informed Finch that there were 4 copies of the book. Seattle Daily Times, February 4, 1926, at 8. No copies have ever been found. A skirmish between the government and the defense at the end of the government's case took place as the government moved to withdraw the book as an exhibit. In fact, the book never had been admitted. Judge Neterer denied the motions and the trial copy of the book remained where it had been for three weeks - in the possession of court clerk Sam Leich. Seattle Daily Times, February 10, 1926, at 8.

[235] Seattle Daily Times, January 28, 1926, at 8.

[236] Seattle Post Intelligencer, January 30, 1926, at 2.

[237] Seattle Daily Times, February 3, 1926, at 8.

[238] Seattle Daily Times, February 3, 1926, at 8.

[239] Metcalfe, at 200.

[240] Seattle Post-Intelligencer, February 5, 1926, at 6.

[241] Metcalfe, at 200. It also may be that there is a paucity of conversations with Elise because she just was not involved in the daily operations of Roy's business regardless of how much she knew.

[242] Seattle Post-Intelligencer, February 4, 1926, at 2. The photograph accompanying the article shows Elise knitting one of the bags.

[243] Seattle Daily Times, February 9, 1926, at 12.

[244] Seattle Daily Times, February 9, 1926, at 1.

[245] Seattle Post-Intelligencer, February 10, 1926, at 1.

[246] Seattle Post-Intelligencer, February 10, 1926, at 1.

[247] Seattle Daily Times, February 10, 1926, at 8.

[248] Seattle Daily Times, February 10, 1926, at 8.

[249] Seattle Daily Times, 12 Feb 1926, at 1.

[250] Seattle Daily Times, February 12, 1926, at 1.

[251] Seattle Daily Times, February 12, 1926, at 11.

[252] Seattle Daily Times, February 12, 1926, at 11.

[253] Seattle Daily Times, February 12, 1926, at 11.

[254] Seattle Daily Times, February 12, 1926, at 11.

[255] Seattle Daily Times, February 12, 1926, at 11.

[256] Seattle Daily Times, February 12, 1926, at 11. We have only the newspaper accounts of the cross-examination to rely on, and the reporter conveying the last questions and answers was not exactly detailed and punctilious about it.

What is clear is that Elise bested McKinney whether or not he had been bribed by Roy to keep Elise out of the case. By this time, she was all the way in it so it is unclear whether any bribe paid to McKinney a year earlier had any influence on his performance.

257 Seattle Daily Times, February 19, 1926, at 1.

258 Seattle Daily Times, February 19, 1926, at 1-2.

259 Seattle Daily Times, February 20, 1926, at 3.

260 Seattle Daily Times, February 21, 1926, at 5.

261 Seattle Daily Times, February 21, 1926, at 1.

262 Seattle Daily Times, February 22, 1926, at 3.

263 Seattle Daily Times, June 7, 1927, at 1.

264 Seattle Union Record, March 4, 1926, at 7.

265 Seattle Daily Times, March 18, 1926, at 16.

266 Seattle Daily Times, May 19, 1926, at 7.

267 Seattle Post-Intelligencer, September 9, 1926, at 5.

268 Seattle Daily Times, April 2, 1926, at 1.

269 Seattle Daily Times, April 2, 1926, at 16. Prosper was released again on bail, but a few months later, he again would be arrested "at sea." The Coast Guard caught him on the speedboat 494-M along with Ed McGinnis, who was convicted with Roy in the Whispering Wires trial and out on bail. A machine gun bullet disabled the motor and the Coast Guard brought them back to Seattle for charges. Seattle Daily Times, October 10, 1926, at 7.

270 Seattle Daily Times, February 22, 1926, at 3. The house was not listed in the classified ads of the newspapers, but remember that Roy's father and his sister Sallie owned Olmsted Realty and were successful real estate brokers. So it is conceivable that the home was on the market "long before" the trial began, but it doesn't really ring true.

271 Seattle Daily Times, February 22, 1926, at 3.

272 Seattle Daily Times, February 22, 1926, at 3.

273 Seattle Daily Times, March 16, 1926, at 27.

274 Almost as if in another life, the Oil-o-Matic Heat Company ran an advert in the Seattle Daily Times inviting readers to ask its customers about how they were enjoying their heating. Among the list of names and addresses was Mrs. Vivian Potter, 3757 Ridgeway. Seattle Daily Times, March 21, 1926, at 37.

275 Seattle Daily Times, March 16, 1926, at 10.

276 Seattle Daily Times, March 16, 1926, at 10.

277 Seattle Daily Times, March 16, 1926, at 10.

278 Seattle Daily Times, March 16, 1926, at 10.

279 Seattle Daily Times, January 14, 1927, at 4.

280 Seattle Daily Times, May 28, 1926, at 1.

281 Seattle Daily Times, January 14, 1927, at 4.

282 Seattle Daily Times, January 14, 1927, at 4.

283 Seattle Daily Times, January 14, 1927, at 4.

284 Seattle Daily Times, May 13, 1926, at 1.

285 Seattle Daily Times, May 13, 1926, at 5.

286 Seattle Post-Intelligencer, May 16, 1926, at 34.

287 Seattle Daily Times, November 19, 1926, at 10.

288 Seattle Daily Times, November 19, 1926, at 10.

289 Seattle Daily Times, November 19, 1926, at 10.

290 The Seattle Star, November 19, 1926, at 6.

291 Seattle Daily Times, November 20, 1926, at 1.

292 Seattle Daily Times, January 20, 1927, at 8.

293 See 19 F.2d 842 (9th Cir. 1927).

294 Seattle Post-Intelligencer, June 9, 1927, at 5.

295 Seattle Post-Intelligencer, October 16, 1927, at 32.

296 Seattle Post-Intelligencer, October 16, 1927, at 32.

297 Seattle Post-Intelligencer, October 16, 1927, at 32.

298 Seattle Post-Intelligencer, October 19, 1927, at 2.

299 Seattle Post-Intelligencer, October 16, 1927, at 32.

300 *See* The Many Lives and Names of a Woman Journalist by Rob Royer, March 1, 2002, at https://crosscut.com/2012/03/the-many-lives-names-woman-journalist

301 Seattle Post-Intelligencer, October 19, 1927, at 2. This is the same picture of Elise and Roy accompanying the article in the newspaper on January 1, 1925, about the end of their halcyon days.

302 Seattle Post-Intelligencer, October 19, 1927, at 2.

303 Seattle Daily Times, October 28, 1927, at 1.

304 Seattle Daily Times, October 28, 1927, at 1.

305 Seattle Daily Times, October 28, 1927, at 1.

306 Seattle Daily Times, October 28, 1927, at 1.

307 Seattle Daily Times, October 28, 1927, at 1,

308 Seattle Daily Times, October 28, 1927, at 2.

309 Seattle Daily Times, November 16, 1927, at 15.

310 Seattle Daily Times, November 16, 1927, at 1.

311 Seattle Post-Intelligencer, November 17, 1927, at 2.

312 Seattle Post-Intelligener, November 17, 1927, at 2.

313 Seattle Daily Times, November 16, 1927, at 1.

314 Seattle Post-Intelligencer, November 17, 1927, at 2. This likely was a reference to McKinney who Roy had bribed early on in exchange for information.

315 Seattle Daily Times, November 16, 1927, at 2.

316 Metcalfe, at 275. Elise's nurse, Mary E. Alexander, also testified to corroborate Roy's testimony. Seattle Post-Intelligencer, November 17, 1927, at 2.

317 Seattle Daily Times, November 21, 1927, at 1.

318 Seattle Daily Times, November 29, 1927, at 5.

319 Seattle Post-Intelligencer, December 1, 1927, at 1.

320 Seattle Post-Intelligencer, December 1, 1927, at 1. One of Elise's grandsons has the portrait.

321 Seattle Post-Intelligencer, December 1, 1927, at 1.

322 Seattle Post-Intelligencer, December 1, 1927, at 1.

323 Seattle Post-Intelligencer, November 30, 1927, at 1.

324 Seattle Post-Intelligencer, November 30, 1927, at 1.

325 Seattle Daily Times, December 8, 1927, at 12.

326 Olmsted Collection. The poem is one of few items that Elise kept from Roy's time in prison. For example, there was no batch of letters to or from prison between them.

327 Prisoners were allowed to write a letter home once a week, and they could receive visitors twice per month on alternate Sundays in the basement of the Administration building where a mesh, floor to ceiling wire screen separated them. Metcalfe, at 321.

328 Seattle Daily Times, December 31, 1927, at 2. Prosper's lawyer condemned Roy for taking advantage of Prosper and his loyalty, saying: "Graignic was a victim of those he worked with and was double crossed until he has not a cent." Seattle Daily Times, December 31, 1927, at 2. Prosper was part of a pioneer family in Washington, raised in boats and on the water. He had a successful career and life after his release, but it is unknown whether he ever had any contact with Roy again. Prosper received an early parole in July 1929 because, he told the court at his sentencing that he "vowed to start anew." The headline

on his release? "Cupid Guides Rum Pilot to Life of Honor." Seattle Daily Times, July 14, 1929. Prosper's vow was out of love for one Eva Fowlis, and they married as soon as he was released. She worked tirelessly for his release and successfully for his honest employment thereafter.

[329] 276 U.S. 609-610 (1928).

[330] Seattle Post-Intelligencer, January 10, 1928, at 1.

[331] Seattle Daily Times, January 10, 1928, at 1.

[332] Seattle Post-Intelligencer, January 31, 1928, at 5.

[333] Seattle Post-Intelligencer, January 31, 1928, at 5.

[334] Seattle Post-Intelligencer, January 31, 1928, at 5.

[335] Seattle Post-Intelligencer, January 31, 1928, at 1.

[336] Seattle Post-Intelligencer, January 31, 1928, at 1.

[337] Seattle Post-Intelligencer, January 31, 1928, at 1

[338] Seattle Daily Times, January 31, 1928, at 9.

[339] Seattle Daily Times, January 31, 1928, at 9.

[340] Seattle Daily Times, February 5, 1928, at 10.

[341] Seattle Post-Intelligencer, February 5, 1928, at 34.

[342] Seattle Post-Intelligencer, February 5, 1928, at 34.

[343] Seattle Post-Intelligencer, February 5, 1928, at 34.

[344] Olmsted Collection, Letter of Paul Bradshaw to Elsie Olmstead dated February 14, 1928. Bradshaw was a forty-year-old insurance investigator and claims adjuster,

married with three children and living in Washington, D.C. He died in 1961. There is no record of how Elise knew him.

[345] Seattle Daily Times, February 6, 1928, at 8.

[346] Seattle Daily Times, May 25, 1928, at 12.

[347] Seattle Daily Times, May 26, 1928, at 5.

[348] Seattle Daily Times, May 26, 1928, at 5. It is very clear that Elise assumed a dominant role in Roy's defense and in formulating the legal strategy going forward with Dore. Over the previous five years, Elise had become intimately acquainted with the legal system and resourceful in raising bonds, dealing with the press, and testifying herself, all in defense of her husband. She was an indomitable advocate for Roy and no doubt would have made an excellent lawyer.

[349] Seattle Daily Times, February 21, 1928, at 1.

[350] Seattle Post-Intelligencer, February 22, 1928, at 3. For a discussion of the Justices' views and the deliberations, as well as the aftermath of the decision, *see Wiretapping on Trial: a case study in the judicial process* by Walter E. Murphy, (Random House, 1965) at 86-103, 121-139.

[351] Seattle Daily Times, March 1, 1928, at 17.

[352] Seattle Daily Times, March 2, 1928, at 1.

[353] Metcalfe, at 283.

[354] Hubbard's career as an agent was over despite being exonerated by the grand jury. Seattle Daily Times, March 23, 1928, at 12.

[355] Seattle Daily Times, March 25, 1928, at 2.

[356] Seattle Daily Times, March 27, 1928, at 2; Seattle Post-Intelligencer, March 28, 1928, at 2.

[357] Seattle Daily Times, March 28, 1928, at 5.

[358] Seattle Post-Intelligencer, March 30, 1928, at 1.

[359] Seattle Post-Intelligencer, May 16, 1928, at 3.

[360] Seattle Post-Intelligencer, May 16, 1928, at 34.

[361] Seattle Daily Times, May 18, 1928, at 13. Ultimately, Elbro and his wife Ruth, Elise's former close friend, did indeed come to live in the U.S. They settled in Mill Valley, California, where they lived out their lives. They had no children.

[362] Seattle Daily Times, March 18, 1928, at 13.

[363] Seattle Daily Times, April 4, 1928, at 1-2.

[364] Seattle Daily Times, June 22, 1928, at 8.

[365] Stockton Evening and Sunday Record, March 8, 1928, at 7.

[366] The Fresno Bee, March 11, 1928, at 34.

[367] Olmsted Collection.

[368] Letter in the Olmsted Collection.

[369] Olmsted Collection.

370 If the shares were acquired or awarded at a ten-cent valuation as the offering suggested, it appears that Roy was trying to double his money.

371 Seattle Daily Times, May 4, 1928, at 26.

372 Seattle Daily Times, May 5, 1928, at 5.

373 Olmsted Collection. The Crown Peak Mine is in Buckhorn Peak in the Bagby-Mariposa-Bullion-Whitlock Mining District. It is in what is known as the Mother Lode gold belt. See https://mindat.org/loc-24207.html.

374 The Fresno Morning Republican newspaper on February 24, 1930, at 12, declared that the Crown Peak mine and other properties belonging to the Butte Boys Mining company are in active development and showing profitable operating values.

375 Olmsted Collection. Both G.W. Bever and H.H. Bever signed the document. As noted, G.W. Bever was president of the company, but it is unclear what relation he is to Harold or presumably H.H. Bever.

376 Seattle Daily Times, August 17, 1930, at 12.

377 Seattle Daily Times, March 19, 1931, at 1.

378 Seattle Post-Intelligencer, November 30, 1927, at 1-2.

379 Seattle Daily Times, June 29, 1928, at 34; *see Wiretapping on Trial: a case study in the judicial process* by Walter E. Murphy, (Random House, 1965) at 125 ("the majority of editorials disapproved of what the Court had done.

Eastern publications were particularly sharp in their comments.")

380 Seattle Daily Times, October 8, 1928, at 1 ("'Whispering Wires' Case Put to Sleep by Supreme Court").

381 Seattle Daily Times, November 17, 1928, at 2.

382 Seattle Daily Times, November 21, 1928, at 13.

383 Seattle Daily Times, November 21, 1928, at 13.

384 Seattle Daily Times, November 21, 1928, at 13.

385 Seattle Daily Times, November 21, 1928, at 13.

386 Interviews with Patricia McFarlane.

387 Metcalfe Letters, July 12, 1993, at 2.

388 Seattle Daily Times, August 17, 1930, at 12.

389 Roy's father died April 17, 1936, and his mother, Sarah Rose, passed away exactly two years to the day later on April 17, 1938. Sarah Rose was a graduate of Boston University. She was an Adventist, so Roy and Elise's lifestyle must have been hard to take during her lifetime. It probably would have been hell for Patricia had she been taken in by them.

390 Olmsted Realty listed dozens of properties for sale each day in the Seattle newspapers.

391 Interviews with Patricia and her sons (2024).

392 Metcalfe, at 321. Metcalfe provided no citation for this assertion. The visitor's book for the penitentiary appears to have been destroyed according to the Seattle NARA, and

the facility's daily logbook contains no reference to visitors generally. Accordingly, we also don't know if Roy's parents, other children, or relatives, except for his two brothers, visited him either.

393 Seattle Post-Intelligencer, October 31, 1929, at 1.

394 Seattle Post-Intelligencer, October 31, 1929, at 1

395 Seattle Post-Intelligencer, October 31, 1929, at 1

396 Seattle Daily Times, November 21, 1928, at 13.

397 Olmsted Collection.

398 Seattle Daily Times, August 17, 1930, at 12. There was the obvious, justifiable bitterness toward Whitney, but it begs the question, why also single out McKinney? While he couldn't deliver on the promise to keep Elise out of the indictment in the Whispering Wires trial, he otherwise had little to do with Elise and her situation. Perhaps the reporter got it wrong and she meant to say U.S. Attorney Revelle or Prohibition head Lyle. It is a mystery.

399 Seattle Daily Times, August 17, 1930, at 12.

400 Metcalfe Letters, July 12, 1993, at 2. Pinkerton has a storied career as an investigative agency. It hired America's first female detective, Kate Warne in 1856. Elise would have been right at home in the agency.

401 Metcalfe, at 305.

402 Seattle Post-Intelligencer, May 20, 1930, at 1.

403 Seattle Daily Times, May 20, 1930, at 1.

404 Seattle Daily Times, May 20, 1930, at 1.

405 Seattle Daily Times, May 20, 1930, at 1.

406 Seattle Post-Intelligencer, May 20, 1930, at 1. Hubbard had concocted an almost laughable story that there was a "directing genius" behind it all, for whom Roy worked, and after Roy's conviction, who directed Hubbard to organize an entirely new ring so that the "stream of profits and 'rake-offs' would go on uninterrupted."

407 Seattle Daily Times, May 20, 1930, at 2.

408 Seattle Daily Times, May 20, 1930, at 1.

409 Los Angeles Examiner, May 29, 1930, at 4.

410 Seattle Post-Intelligencer, May 21, 1930, at 1.

411 Seattle Post-Intelligencer, May 27, 1930, Section 2, at 1.

412 San Francisco Chronicle, June 4, 1930, at 3.

413 The Seattle Star, June 5, 1930, at 1.

414 San Francisco Evening Tribune, June 13, 1930, at 8.

415 Seattle Daily Times, June 20, 1930, at 7.

416 San Francisco Evening Tribune, June 19, 1930, at 35. The Seattle Post-Intelligencer carried the transcript of the hearing and the story the same day on page 1. Seattle Post-Intelligencer, June 19, 1930, at 1.

417 Seattle Daily Times, June 20, 1930, at 7.

418 Seattle Daily Times, June 28, 1930, at 2.

419 Seattle Post-Intelligencer, August 18, 1930, at 1, 3.

420 San Francisco Chronicle, August 26, 1930, at 5.

421 Seattle Post-Intelligencer, August 26, 1930, at 2.

422 Seattle Post-Intelligencer, August 26, 1930, at 2.

423 Seattle Post-Intelligencer, September 21, 1930, at 1.

424 Chattanooga Times Free Press, August 26, 1930, at 3.

425 Seattle Daily Times, September 3, 1930, at 10.

426 Seattle Post-Intelligencer, May 13, 1931, at 2.

427 Seattle Post-Intelligencer, May 12, 1931, at 1.

428 Seattle Daily Times, May 25, 1931, at 2.

429 See NARA, Pardon File. Frank and Ralph most certainly were NOT the principal owners of the mine. One wonders if in fact they owned any shares at all or more likely, held Roy shares under their names.

430 See NARA, Pardon File.

431 Seattle Post-Intelligencer, December 25, 1935, at 1.

432 From May 1931 to July 1932, Roy and Elise and Patricia resided at the Northcliffe Apartment Hotel on 1119 Boren Avenue. From August 1932 to April 1933, they lived in the Rhododendron Apartment Hotel at 1006 Spring Street. From May 1933 to June 1934, they lived in the Marlborough Apartments at 1220 Boren Avenue, and then at the Wilsonian Apartments at 4710 University Street.

433 Seattle Post-Intelligencer, December 25, 1935, at 1.

434 Seattle Post-Intelligencer, December 25, 1935, at 1.

435 Metcalfe, at 340.

436 Seattle Post-Intelligencer, May 6, 1966, at 28.

437 Seattle Daily Times, April 6, 1934, at 9.

438 Seattle Daily Times, May 9, 1934, at 3.

439 Seattle Daily Times, April 12, 1934, at 3.

440 Seattle Daily Times, March 19, 1935, at 2.

441 Seattle Post-Intelligencer, November 13, 1938, at 2.

442 Olmsted Collection. A copy of the FBI letter is held by the author.

443 Olmsted Collection. A copy of the application is on file with the author.

444 See https://pipesmagazine.com/forums/threads/corn-cob-pipe-club-of-virginia.32500/

445 Likely the remaining park and exhibits from Century of Progress International Exposition, also known as the Chicago World's Fair, which was held in Chicago from 1933 to 1934.

446 Metcalfe, at 342. The 1940 Census shows Roy living in a boarding house on John Street in Seattle without Elise. He earned $2100 the prior year as a salesman.

447 Seattle Post-Intelligencer, August 5, 1943, at 3.

448 Seattle Post-Intelligencer, August 5, 1943, at 3.

449 Interview with Patricia McFarlane.

450 Seattle Post-Intelligencer, September 8, 1940, at 1.

451 https://www.britannica.com/event/the-Blitz

452 While we know that Elise's sister Lily and her brother Carl had found Elise in the late 1930s, we have no correspondence or other records to know how frequently, if at all, they remained in contact by mail or telephone. Patricia made the trek to Philadelphia to visit Lily, but we know nothing more of their relationships.

453 *What Happened in Seattle after Pearl Harbor,* The Seattle Times, December 7, 2016, updated December 7, 2021, available at https://www.seattletimes.com/seattle-news/northwest/dark-days-in-seattle-as-pearl-harbor-attack-begins-75-years-ago/

454 The Port was established in January 1942 and became one of the busiest during the War, critical for moving troops and supplies overseas. See https://www.historylink.org/File/10986. In applying, Elise had letters of recommendation written in October 1942 from two City Counsel members and the Mayor. The last four years of her work for the City were in the Traffics Violations Bureau, directly under the supervision of William J. Devin, who became mayor of Seattle in 1942. These letters are among the Olmsted Collection.

455 Olmsted Collection.

456 In May 2013, the Seattle Post-Intelligencer shared previously unpublished photographs of World War II in Seattle. The photographs were donated by the paper to the

Seattle Museum of History and Industry ("MOHAI"). Among the photographs, the paper commented, "probably the best moment captured from the blackout events involved Harold Mouser and Lenore Frank. According to notes preserved at MOHAI, the couple was 17 and 16 when the newspaper photographer saw them on Dec. 8, 1941 – the day after the Pearl Harbor attack. The pair were at a restaurant and when the lights went out, Mouser got a kiss. That image, captured in the dark with a flash camera, has become one of the most memorable images in the collection. The couple later married and had five children, according to MOHAI. When the picture ran in the newspaper decades later, someone called to identify them." https://www.seattlepi.com/local/seattle-history/article/world-war-ii-in-seattle-previously-unpublished-4496994.php

[457] Patricia graduated from Broadway High School in 1943. Patricia's photo in the 1942 yearbook was all smiles. The school had the largest number of Japanese students of all the schools in Seattle, approximately 25% of the school in 1942. The forced removal of Japanese in Seattle greatly impacted the school whose overall population declined to the point that the 1946 graduating class was its last one. *See* https://www.historylink.org/File/10475. She would go on to get her degree in Sociology from University of Washington, marry Donald McFarlane, and have three children. She later divorced in 1969.

458 The 2011 Ken Burns documentary is called, appropriately enough, *Prohibition: A Nation of Scofflaws*, and Patricia appears in the second episode.

459 Seattle Daily Times, June 27, 1941, at 1; Seattle Post-Intelligencer, June 28, 1941, at 3.

460 Metcalfe Letters, July 12, 1993, at 2.

461 Frank Jr. was attached to Marine Fighting Squadron 218, MAG-14, known as the "Hellions." They departed the United States in December 1943 on board the carrier USS Barnes and arrived at Espiritu Santo in the New Hebrides on January 5, 1944. They flew missions against the Japanese stronghold on Rabaul. He was first listed as missing in action in June and confirmed as killed in action on July 18, 1944. Seattle Daily Times, July 18, 1944, at 5.

462 Seattle Daily Times, December 21, 1946, at 3.

463 Florence eventually moved to Seattle from Chicago, and she died in 1949 without children.

464 Seattle Daily Times, December 21, 1946, at 3.

465 Seattle Daily Times, December 23, 1946, at 2.

466 Seattle Post-Intelligencer, December 22, 1946, at 30.

467 Seattle Post-Intelligencer, May 6, 1966, at 28.

468 Clark's notes of the interview, if any, cannot be found so we don't know if she simply had nothing to say or wouldn't discuss things. But the fact that Clark got wrong the singularly important fact that Elise was a government

informant suggests that either Roy, Elise or both misled him about Elise's role in Roy's business.

[469] Metcalfe Letters, July 12, 1993, at 2.

[470] Metcalfe Letters, May 28, 1993, at 2.

[471] The Seattle Times, March 9, 1979, at 55.

[472] Available at https://archive.org/details/cu31924029843244 or HathiTrust at https://hdl.handle.net/2027/coo1.ark:/13960/t0wq0jk1t. [hereinafter "Olmsted Genealogy"]. Roy's direct line begins on page 302 of the book.

[473] Olmsted Genealogy at 5.

[474] The Olmste(a)d Family Association maintains a website at www.olmsteadfamily.org, a Facebook page, publishes a newsletter and employs a staff genealogist and archivist for the family history. They sponsor Olmsted reunions across the country periodically.

[475] Olmsted Genealogy at 189.

[476] Olmsted Genealogy at 193.

[477] The quotation comes from an entry on Ancestry.com for Ebenezer, quoting Tim Abbott, a writer and descendant of Ebenezer's.

[478] On the strength of Ebenezer's Revolutionary War service, Roy could have joined the Sons of the American Revolution. But Roy probably didn't know a thing about his family history. One of Roy's grandsons today is a

beneficiary of this history and has been accepted into the Sons of the American Revolution as a result.

[479] The quotation comes from an entry on Ancestry.com for Ebenezer, quoting Tim Abbott, a writer and descendant of Ebenezer's. *See also Ebenezer Olmsted: Tax Collector Who Broke the Town,* May 2, 2018, available at http://www.naturegeezer.com/2018/05/p_91.html

[480] From the obituary of his grandson, Henry W. Olmsted, The Hastings Daily Tribune, Dec. 13, 1922 at 6.

[481] Prophetstown was named after an Indian "prophet" who was an advisor to Black Hawk, a Sauk chief and warrior. The town occupied the lands of the Winnebago people who had abandoned the land after the Black Hawk War.